CRITTERS

EDITORS
Judith Hillen
Arthur Wiebe
Dave Youngs

AUTHORS
Maureen Murphy Allen
Debby Deal
Gale Philips Kahn
Suzanne Scheidt
Vincent Sipkovich

ILLUSTRATORS
Max Cantu
Doug Castleman
Lori Esau
Lori Hammeras
Brenda Howsepian
Cheryl Johnson
Gail Linenbach
Ellen Small
Amy Todd
Dee Vlasak

AIMS (**A**ctivities **I**ntegrating **M**athematics and **S**cience) began in 1981 with a grant from the National Science Foundation. The non-profit AIMS Education Foundation publishes hands-on instructional materials (books and the monthly AIMS Newsletter) that integrate curricular disciplines such as mathematics, science, language arts, and social studies. The Foundation sponsors a national program of professional development through which educators may gain both an understanding of the AIMS philosophy and expertise in teaching by integrated, hands-on methods.

Copyright ©1992 by the AIMS Education Foundation

All rights reserved. No part of this work may be reproduced or transmitted in any form or by any means—graphic, electronic, or mechanical, including photocopying, taping, or information storage/retrieval systems—without written permission of the publisher unless such copying is expressly permitted by federal copyright law. The following are exceptions to the foregoing statements:

- A person or school purchasing this AIMS publication is hereby granted permission to make up to 200 copies of any portion of it, provided these copies will be used for educational purposes and only at that school site.

- An educator providing a professional development workshop is granted permission to make up to 35 copies of student activity sheets or enough to use the lessons one time with one group.

Schools, school districts, and other non-profit educational agencies may purchase duplication rights for one or more books for use at one or more school sites. Contact the AIMS Education Foundation for specific, current information. Address inquiries to Duplication Rights, AIMS Education Foundation, P.O. Box 8120, Fresno, CA 93747-8120.

ISBN 1-881431-23-1

Printed in the United States of America

Table of Contents

Getting Started
- Parent Letter 1
- A Collecting We Will Go 2
- Vocabulary List 3
- Home on the Range 4
- Animal Antics 8

Insects and Spiders
- Insects (fact sheet) 16
- Spiders (fact sheets) 17
- Wings 'N' Webs 19
- Popping Through the Garden 25

Mealworms
- Mealworms (fact sheets) 29
- My Mealworm 31
- Mealworms on Stage 35

Earthworms
- Warming Up to Worms 39
- Earthworms (fact sheets) 43
- Worm Home 52
- Reaction to Light 53
- Reaction to Touch 54
- Reaction to Moisture 55
- Now You See Them, Now You Don't 56

Snails
- Observations 58
- Snails (fact sheets) 60
- Inside Out 69
- Portrait of an Average Snail 72
- The Slime Trail 76
- The Up or Down Snail 80
- What's Your Angle 82
- Snail Olympics 84

Silkworms
- Silkworms (fact sheets) 88
- Growing Pains 91

Isopods
- Isopods 95
- Hot Foot, Cold Foot 96

Aquatic Critters
- Fishful Thinking 101
- Fishing for Fins 103
- Brine Shrimp 108

Adaptation and Camouflage
- Table Manners 111
- Under Cover 115
- Hide and Seek 120
- Gone Fishing 124
- Missing Moths 128
- Moth Maps 131

Food Chains
- Food Chains 134
- Catch Me If You Can 136

Other
- Census Takers 139
- Who's Home in the Biome 142
- Critter Trivia Ideas 150

Index of Skills

Math

Adding	41,47,73,84
Averaging	36,49,61,65,71,79,109,124
Comparing	36,39,61,79,109,124
Counting	26,36,61,79,109,121
Using decimals	116
Dviding	71,73
Using equations	71,79,121
Estimating	84,96,105,113,116,124
Fractions	47,105,109,116
Graphing	8,36,61,65,71,84,100,109,113,116,124
Using matrices	79,116
Measuring	32,39,58,61,65,68,71,73,79,84,105
Multiplying	8,43,65,121
Using percentage	53,55,116
Problem solving	65,84
Sampling	124
Sequencing	109
Subtracting	47

Science

Observing	all activities
Classifying	4,8,20,26,32,61,84,96,100,127
Predicting	39,61,65,71,79,84,96,105,109,124
Collecting and recording data	all activities
Measuring	32,60,61,65,71,73,79,84,105
Applying and generalizing	all activities
Hypothesizing	all activities

I HEAR, AND I FORGET
I SEE, AND I REMEMBER
I DO, AND I UNDERSTAND

—Chinese Proverb

Dear Parents

Our class will be doing a number of hands-on math/science activities. These life science activities involve a variety of critters ie. insects, snails, etc... The activities combine science processes with mathematical skills.

The critter activities will require a number of materials. We would greatly appreciate your contribution of any of the materials listed below. Please send the materials that you are willing to donate to school by _____.
　　　　　　　　　　　　　　　　　　　　　　date

Thank-you very much,

_____ teacher

_____ child

Materials List

- 2 liter soda bottles
- 1g. jar with lid
- ½ gal. milk carton
- plastic shoebox
- animal cookies
- goldfish crackers
- gummy worms
- gravel
- clear plastic cups (10 oz.)
- toilet paper tubes
- feathers
- wax paper
- popsicle sticks
- toothpicks
- egg cartons
- marshmallows
- yarn
- sandwich baggies (ziploc)
- mulberry leaves
- aluminum foil
- baby food jars

CRITTERS　　　　　1　　　　　©1989 AIMS Education Foundation

A Collecting We Will Go...

Snails...

Snails can be found early in the morning and late at night in moist spots in your yard. They are underneath and on the sides of moist leaves and walls. To make a snail catcher, use a square of black or brown trash bag, set it on top of moist ground for 2 days. Collect the snails in the early morning or evening; they will be underneath the plastic.

Isopods...

Isopods can be found in cool, moist locations. They are under wood, clumps of ground cover, and rocks. To make an isopod collector, hollow out a potato and set it in a cool, moist location overnight.

Mealworms...

Mealworms can be purchased at any pet shop or fish bait store. If you want them to remain in the larval stage, refrigerate them. Otherwise, at room temperature, the life cycle will continue.

Earthworms...

Earthworms can be found on the surface after a rain or by digging in rich, moist soil. Another way to obtain earthworms is to purchase them at a pet shop or bait shop. (Note: earthworms are often called "nightcrawlers".)

Brine Shrimp...

Brine shrimp can be purchased at a toy store or pet shop.

Goldfish...

Goldfish can be purchased at any pet shop. Be sure to ask about your local water, dechlorinators are often required.

CRITTERS ©1989 AIMS Education Foundation

CRITTERS
Vocabulary List

abdomen: the last section of an insect's 3 main body parts

adapt: changing to fit the environment

antennae: (singular; antenna) the sensory organs of an insect — Antennae are used to smell, taste, feel, and sometimes hear.

biome: ecosystems that have similar wildlife, climates and vegetation

camouflage: an organism's ability to blend in with the environment

carnivore: animal that eats meat

census: the counting of a population

chrysalis: the pupal case of many butterflies

cold-blooded: an animal that cannot maintain a constant body temperature independent of the outside temperature — Insects, reptiles, fish, and amphibians are cold-blooded.

cocoon: the pupal case of many moths that is made out of a silk like material

consumer: higher level organisms that get their food from other living things

gills: organs in fish that separate dissolved oxygen from water

habitat: the environment in which an animal lives

herbivore: animal that eats only plants

invertebrate: animals without backbones

larva: (plural; larvae) the second stage of an insect that goes through complete metamorphosis (i.e., egg-larva-pupa-adult) — Insect larvae look very different from the adults. For example, moth or butterfly larvae are caterpillars, fly larvae are maggots, and beetle larvae are grubs.

life cycle: series of stages through which an organism passes.

metamorphosis: the stages of development through which an organism changes its body form

molt: to shed the outer skin or exoskeleton. As an insect grows, it sheds its skin several times before it reaches the adult stage.

nymph: the immature stage of an insect that goes through incomplete or simple metamorphosis — It looks like the adult but is much smaller.

omnivore: animal that eats both plants and animals

population: total number of organisms of one species in a particular area

predator: animal that eats other animals

prey: animal that serves as food for another animal

producer: green plants that are able to make their own food

pupa: (plural; pupae) the inactive stage of an insect that goes through complete metamorphosis — The larva changes into a pupa, and then becomes an adult.

spider: an arthropod that has 2 main body parts, 8 legs, and fangs — Spiders are related to insects.

thorax: the middle section of an insect's body to which the legs and wings are attached

vertebrate: animals with backbones

warm-blooded: animals that are able to maintain a constant body temperature independent of the outside temperature — Birds and mammals are warm-blooded.

HOME ON THE RANGE

I. **Topic Area**
   Critter homes

II. **Introductory Statement**
   Students will identify several critters and their environmental needs and assign them to appropriate homes.

III. **Math Skills**   **Science Processes**
   a. Observing
   b. Collecting & organizing data
   c. Classifying
   d. Inferring
   e. Applying

IV. **Materials**
   activity sheets
   scissors
   glue
   crayons
   materials to make critter homes

V. **Key Question**
   What would be needed to build a suitable, humane home for critters?

VI. **Background Information**
   Students are fascinated by critters and often want to keep them in a jar or box with inadequate ventilation and no food or water. They need to be taught that even small animals like isopods and ants have needs and should be treated humanely. This activity is meant to make students aware of the kind of homes that would provide a good environment for various critters. These homes can easily be constructed from inexpensive materials. Below is a description of the four homes pictured on the activity sheets.
   1. Two liter plastic bottle home — soil & cupful of water
      butterfly, lizard, ant, tarantula, snake, snail
   2. Jar home — branch, gravel and a cup of water
      butterfly, snake, lizard, tarantula, ant
   3. Milk carton home — oatmeal and a slice of potato
      mealworm, isopods
   4. Plastic shoebox-aquarium home — water and a rock
      fish, tadpole, turtle, aquatic snails

VII. **Management Suggestions**
   1. Have a selection of small animals and their homes available for the students to observe, if possible, to help stimulate class discussion about suitable critter homes. These could be things like fish in a bowl or aquarium, ants in an ant farm, a bird in its cage, etc.
   2. The inexpensive homes recorded on "Home on the Range" are suggested for use as classroom critter homes and if possible, an example of each should be available for students to examine.
   3. This activity can be done in one or two days. The students can do this as a paper and pencil activity or they can actually build one of the homes.

VIII. **Procedure**
   1. Discuss the key question and talk about the things that must be considered in order to safely and humanely keep small animals in the classroom.
   2. Talk about each home on the "Find Me a Home" activity sheet. Have students select the critters that can live together and discuss what homes would be appropriate for them. They can cut out the pictures of the critters and paste them on an appropriate home.
   3. "Home on the Range" shows four easy to make, inexpensive critter homes. Discuss these homes and their features. Working in teams or individually, students can design an additional critter home and draw a picture of it on the activity sheet.
   4. Students can build one of the four homes or one of their own design. The teacher may want to have a collection of materials available for students to work with, such as milk cartons, juice cans, plastic juice bottles, nylon stocking, rubber bands, tape, shoeboxes, etc.
   5. If homes are built to keep live critters, students must provide their critters with the proper care.

IX. **Discussion Questions**
   1. What would happen if you put the lizard in the milk carton?
   2. Which other critters must have specific homes? Why?
   3. Which critters could live in any of the homes? Why?
   4. Besides creating a safe home for class pets what else is important in their environment?
   5. How could a critter's need for food and water be met in each of the homes?

X. **Extended Activities**
   1. Research a particular critter and report your findings.
   2. Use the "You won't believe what's in my jar!" page and write a story.

Home on the Range

Use a 2-liter bottle with base removed. Cut off the top of the bottle, turn over, and place inside the base. Poke holes in the top with a nail.

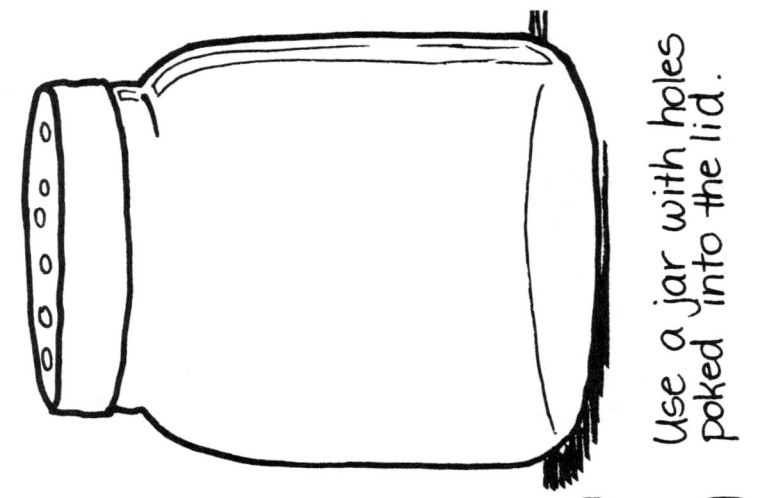

Use a jar with holes poked into the lid.

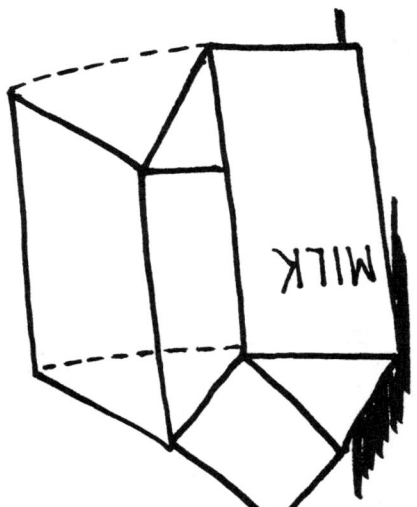

Use a milk carton with one side cut off. If you need a lid, use plastic wrap poked with holes, and tape down.

Use a plastic shoebox. If a lid is needed, an adult can use a hot nail to poke holes in the plastic lid.

Design a new critter home that is easy to build......

_____ loves to live in this home!

CRITTERS   6   ©1989 AIMS Education Foundation

ANIMAL ANTICS

I. **Topic Area**
   Animal classification

II. **Introductory Statement**
   Students will sort animals into appropriate classifications in the Animal Kingdom.

III. **Math Skills**
   a. Graphing
   b. Computation

   Science Processes
   a. Observing
   b. Classifying and sorting

IV. **Materials**
   activity sheets
   classification chart
   bags containing any or all of the following:
      animal cookies, duck or goldfish crackers, gummy worms, plastic bugs, spiders, snakes, lizards and pictures of animals

V. **Key Question**
   How do scientists classify animals?

VI. **Background Information**
   The Animal Kingdom can be classified into two groups, the vertebrates and the invertebrates. Vertebrates are animals with a backbone and can be classified into five sub groups: mammals, birds, fish, reptiles and amphibians. The invertebrates are classified into *many groups*, but for this activity will only be sorted into four sub groups: ringed worms, arthropods (insects, spiders, crabs), mollusks (slugs, squid, snails) and echinoderms (spiny skinned animals like starfish, sea urchins and sand dollars). This activity is dealing with classification on an elementary level and is not intended to be complete, but rather to expose elementary students to the idea of classifying animals into groups according to attributes they have in common. Likewise, this activity may be too complex for primary students, but a creative teacher can use the pictures and have students sorting and classifying on a more primary level.

VII. **Management Suggestions**
   1. This activity can be done as a game as described below or simply as a sorting exercise using the animal pictures and the fact sheets to classify animals.
   2. A sheet of animal pictures is included with the activity. It may be duplicated to provide animal pictures for the class to sort and classify.
   3. Each group will get a bag containing as many animals (animal pictures, toys, cookies, etc.) as possible to sort.
   4. The Animal Kingdom fact sheets can be used to help students who are not familiar with animal classification.
   5. The classification chart used for this activity is on two pages that need to be run off separately and taped together. Each group will need a chart.

VIII. **Procedure**
   1. Each team is given a bag containing approximately the same number of animals to sort.
   2. Let the students look at the animals they have in the bag for a few minutes and then return the animals to the bag.
   3. Pass out the activity sheets and chart and explain that the object of the game is to correctly sort the animals according to the classification system given on the chart.
   4. Discuss the point system for the game as given on the data sheet. Have students predict how many points they think they will get and record their prediction on the data sheet.
   5. Have the team place the animals at the top of the chart in the section marked "All Animals" and count them. Record this number on the data sheet.
   6. The team will then divide their animals into two groups (vertebrates and invertebrates) on the chart. Check the teams for correct placement. One point for each correct placement is given and recorded on the data sheet.
   7. The team will then sort the vertebrates into one of five categories on the chart. The teacher will check for correct placement and points are then calculated for all the correct classifications. For example, if the team correctly classified 3 reptiles, they will get 3 × 4 or 12 points and record these points on the data sheet.
   8. The same procedure is followed for the invertebrates.
   9. After each team has calculated its score, the scores of all the teams can be recorded and graphed on the graphing page.

IX. **Discussion Questions**
   1. What do the mammals have in common? The reptiles? The mollusks? etc.
   2. Was your predicted score close to your team's score? Why or why not?
   3. Which group of animals is most often selected as pets? Why do you think this is so?
   4. How would you sort the mammals into smaller categories?
   5. Can you devise an animal classification system that is different from the one given on the chart?

X. **Extended Activities**
   1. A large classification chart can be drawn on butcher paper and placed on a bulletin board. Each student can cut out and color an animal picture and paste it on the chart in the appropriate place.
   2. Older students can find the ratios or percents of animals they had in each category on the chart.
   3. Younger students can do the activity with only the animal pictures and sort them any way they want.

XI. **Curriculum Coordinates**
   Art:
   Use the cut out animals to make a zoo picture.
   Creative Writing:
   Students can write an animal story. The "Just So Stories" by Rudyard Kipling are great for ideas. You can read "The Elephant's Child" story from Kipling's book about how the elephant got its trunk and then have students write their own stories about how animals got their unique features.
   Research:
   Students can research other animal classification systems or find other invertebrate classes that were not included on the chart in this lesson.

ANIMAL KINGDOM

Animals can be classified into 2 groups. The Vertebrates are animals with a backbone. The Invertebrates are animals without a backbone. Run your hand down your back. Do you feel the bumpy bones? That is your backbone. You are a vertebrate.

There are 5 groups of Vertebrates:
- mammals — warm blooded animals that have hair or fur and are born alive.
- birds — warm blooded animals that have feathers and lay eggs.
- fish — cold blooded animals that have scales, gills, and fins and lay eggs.
- reptiles — cold blooded animals that have scales, and lungs and lay eggs.
- amphibians — cold blooded animals that have a smooth skin and can live on land or in water.

Warm blooded animals have a constant body temperature. Cold blooded animals have a body temperature that adjusts to the temperature of their environment.

ANIMAL ANTICS

ANIMAL

Vertebrates

mammals
1 point

reptiles
4 points

birds
2 points

amphibians
5 points

fish
3 points

CRITTERS ©1992 AIMS Education Foundation

Animal Antics

Kingdom

Invertebrates

"Wonder where I belong?"

mollusks
4 points

annelids
1 point

echinoderms
3 points

arthropods
2 points

ANIMAL KINGDOM

There are many groups of Invertebrates. Here are four of the main ones.

- annelids — cold blooded animals that have a soft body with sections.
- echinoderms — cold blooded animals that have bodies with rough skin and sharp spines.
- mollusks — cold blooded animals with a soft body and sometimes a hard shell.
- arthropods — cold blooded animals with jointed legs.

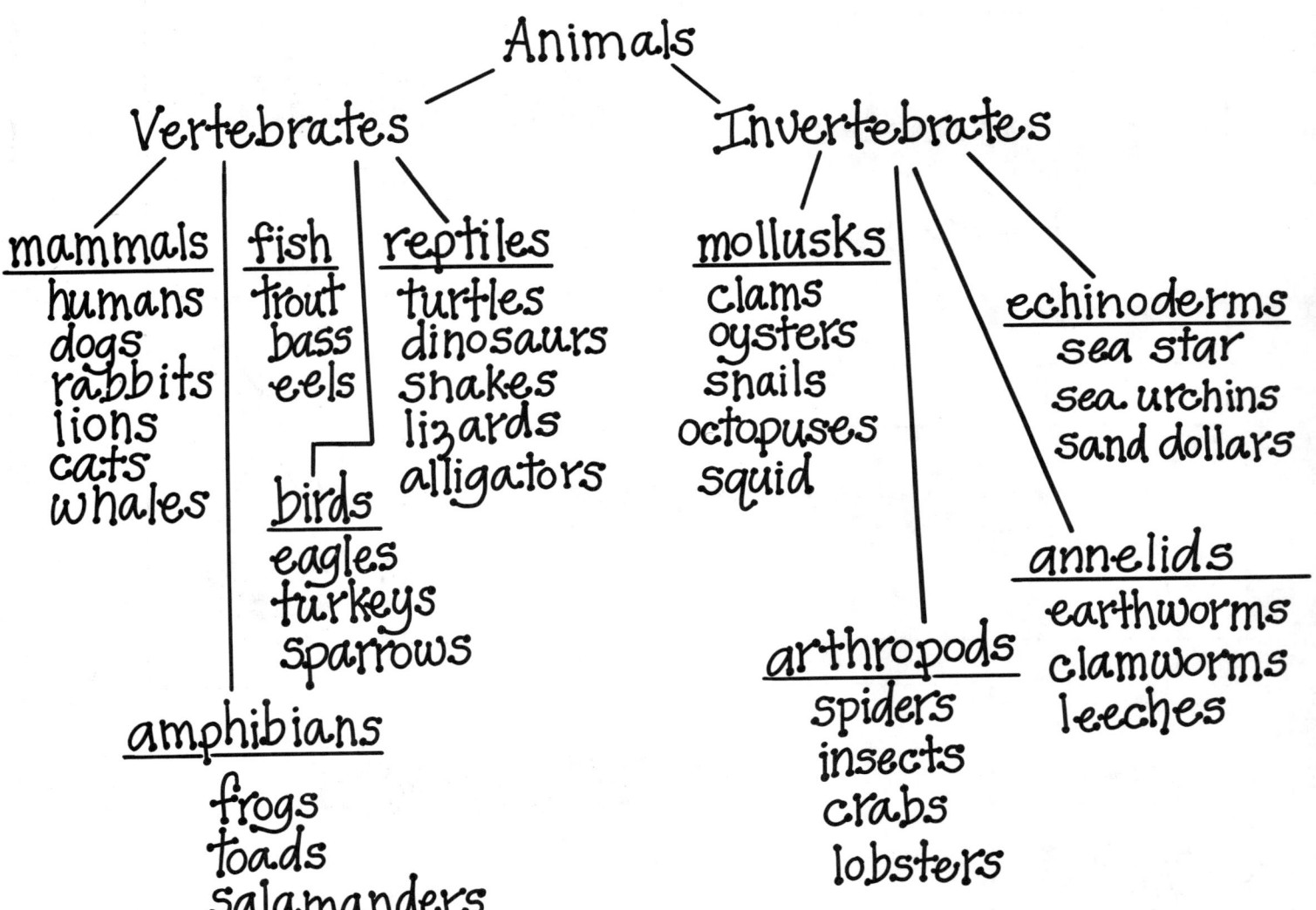

Animal Antics
Data Sheet

Team Members
_____
_____
_____

Prediction:

We think we will earn _____ points.

| All Animals | _____ |

| Vertebrates | _____ |
| Invertebrates | _____ |

Points Earned

mammals	_____	×	1	=	_____
fish	_____	×	3	=	_____
birds	_____	×	2	=	_____
reptiles	_____	×	4	=	_____
amphibians	_____	×	5	=	_____
annelids	_____	×	1	=	_____
mollusks	_____	×	4	=	_____
arthropods	_____	×	2	=	_____
echinoderms	_____	×	3	=	_____

TEAM TOTAL

CRITTERS   13   ©1989 AIMS Education Foundation

Name _____

Finding the Animal Antics Winner

Record the scores:

Team	1	2	3	4	5	6	7	8
Score								

 **Now graph the scores:**

1	2	3	4	5	6	7	8

Teams

Winning Team →

CRITTERS ©1989 AIMS Education Foundation

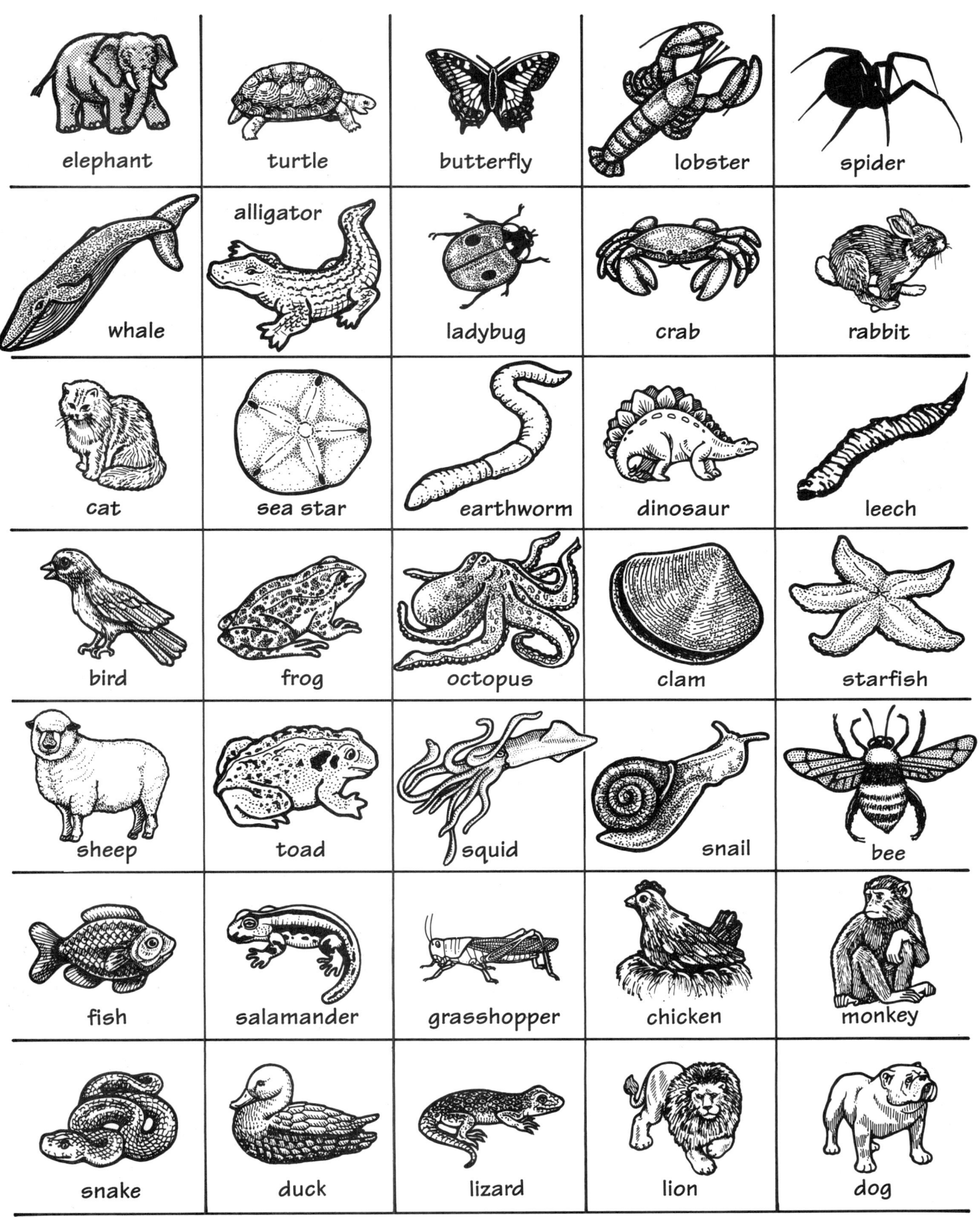

Insects

The major role of the insect is pollination, which is very necessary to the plants and animals of the earth. Insects also eat other insects, carry disease and can cause destruction of crops and whole fields.

Insects have been on earth for over 300 million years. There are more insects than all other animals put together.

Insects belong to the class Insecta, among the Arthropods. Arthropoda means "jointed legs". Their relatives are spiders, crabs and lobsters, and centipedes and millipedes.

Insects have three body parts: the head, the thorax or chest, and the abdomen or hind body. They have six legs. Most insects have wings and two compound eyes, though there may be a number of small simple eyes. Most have antennae for smelling. Insects have a hard exterior skeleton, or exoskeleton.

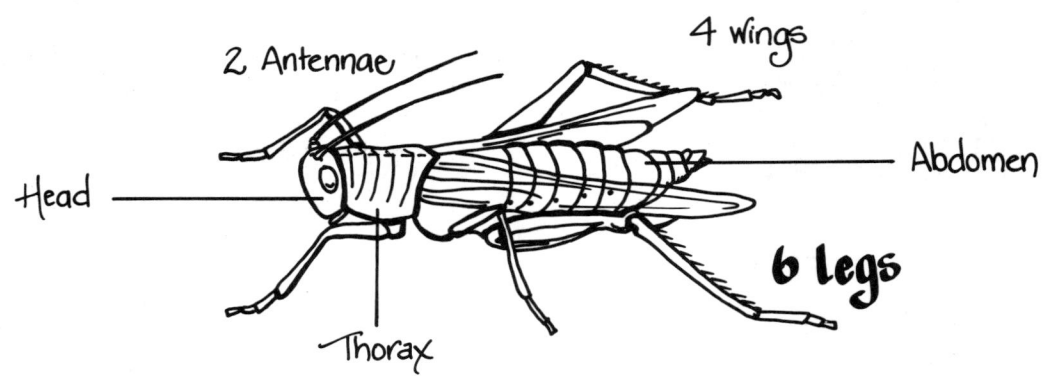

Most insects go through a life pattern called metamorphosis: caterpillar to moth, or maggot to fly. There are four major groups of insects: BEETLES, BUTTERFLIES and MOTHS, WASPS, BEES and ANTS, FLIES, MOSQUITOS and GNATS. "Entomologists" study insects, and have probably discovered and identified only about half of these important creatures.

Spiders

The major role of the spider is to eat insects. Every year they do away with millions and millions of insects that destroy grain crops and eat green leaves. Most spiders are timid, harmless, and quite helpful. The two spiders to watch out for are the black widow and the brown recluse spider, which are harmful to humans.

Spiders have been on earth for hundreds of millions of years. They are numerous, and found everywhere except Antarctica.

More than 30,000 different species are known. Over 2,000 of these live in the United States.

Spiders belong to the phylum Arthropoda as do insects. Their class is Arachnida and the order of spiders is Araneae. The word Arachnida comes from a Greek myth. Arachne lived in Greece many centuries ago. Her spinning and weaving was so skilled, that she challenged Athena, the goddess of weaving and handicrafts, to a contest. Her tapestry was so perfect that, according to the story, Athena became enraged and turned her into a spider, condemning her to perpetual spinning. Our word 'spider' comes from the German word 'spinner', meaning one who spins.

Spiders have an exoskeleton like insects. They have eight legs. The spider's body has two parts: the head and thorax (cephalothorax) are one part, the abdomen is the second. There are no wings and no antennae or feelers. A spider usually has eight simple eyes. Spiders molt (shed their outer covering) during growth, rather than go through a metamorphosis. Most live about one year, but tarantulas may live 20 years.

A spider does not chew its food. It paralyzes or kills its prey with its fangs and then a digestive juice turns the tissues into a liquid which is then sucked into the spider's stomach.

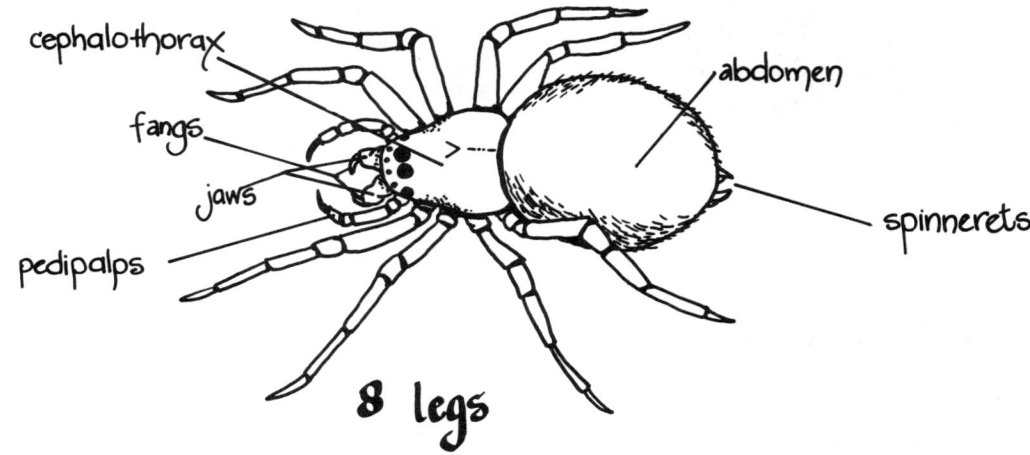

Spiders produce silk from glands in their bodies. As the liquid shoots out of six spinnerets and is exposed to the air, it hardens. The spinnerets control and shape the silk which can be thin, thick, dry, sticky, soft, stretchy or beaded. The spider uses the silk for webs, traps, nests, to wrap, and also as a dragline. Females wrap their eggs with silk. Spiderlings release silk and use it to carry themselves in the wind. This is called ballooning.

Spider silk has been used by primitive people for fishing nets, lures, bags, and headdresses. The silk has also been used as cross hairs in astronomical telescopes, levels, and surveying equipment.

WINGS 'N WEBS

I. **Topic Area**
   Insects and spiders

II. **Introductory Statement**
   Students will learn external differences in the bodies of insects and spiders by observing and constructing.

III. **Math Skills**
   a. Tables
   b. Counting
   c. Whole numbers
   d. Graphing

   Science Processes
   a. Observing
   b. Collecting and recording data
   c. Organizing data
   d. Drawing conclusions
   e. Generalizing
   f. Comparing

IV. **Materials**
   An insect and spider for each group (the pictures provided in this investigation may be used if necessary).
   Hand lenses
   Pipe cleaners — ten pieces two inches long for each student
   Tooth picks — five per student
   Clay — 50 grams per student
   Construction paper — 3"x3" per student, any color
   Scissors
   Activity sheets

V. **Key Question**
   What are the external differences between the bodies of insects and spiders?

VI. **Background Information**
   See data sheets.

VII. **Management Suggestions**
   1. Each group of children needs an insect and a spider. It is very important that "real" specimens be provided by teacher or students. If this is not possible, fill in with the pictures provided in the investigation.
   2. Work in groups of 4-5 students.

VIII. **Procedure**
   1. Divide students into groups of 4 or 5.
   2. Give each group a spider and an insect. If these are not available give each group a picture of each.
   3. Each student is given activity sheets.
   4. Each student will record the name of the insect and spider used in his group.
   5. Students will compare the insect and spider and record observations on the table.
   6. The class will discuss findings.
   7. All students will write a sentence or two about the differences observed.
   8. Now that students know some of the differences, they will finish the drawings.
   9. Students will each make an insect or spider out of clay, tooth picks, pipe cleaners, and construction paper.
   10. Students will make a drawing of their creation, label it a spider or insect, and name it.
   11. Students will guess each other's creation and record on table.
   12. Class will build a real graph on the floor of spiders and insects using their own creations, and then make a block graph of their own.
   13. Discuss.

IX. **Discussion Questions**
   1. What are the differences in the bodies of insects and spiders?
   2. Have you seen creatures which are not insects or spiders but which appear very similar?

X. **Extended Activities**
   1. Collect insects and spiders and identify.
   2. Make a booklet of one spider or insect.

XI. **Curriculum Coordinates**
   1. Creative Writing: Write a make-believe story about a spider or insect.
   2. Geography: What is the territory of certain insects or spiders?
   3. Literature: Books to read — Anansi Tales and Charlotte's Web.
   4. History:
      a. How are spiders and insects used to represent good and evil in past civilizations?
      b. How have insects caused crop damage and to what historical significance?
      c. Why do states inspect fruits and vegetables at borders?

Wings 'n Webs

Name: _____

Common name of your insect: _____ Spider: _____

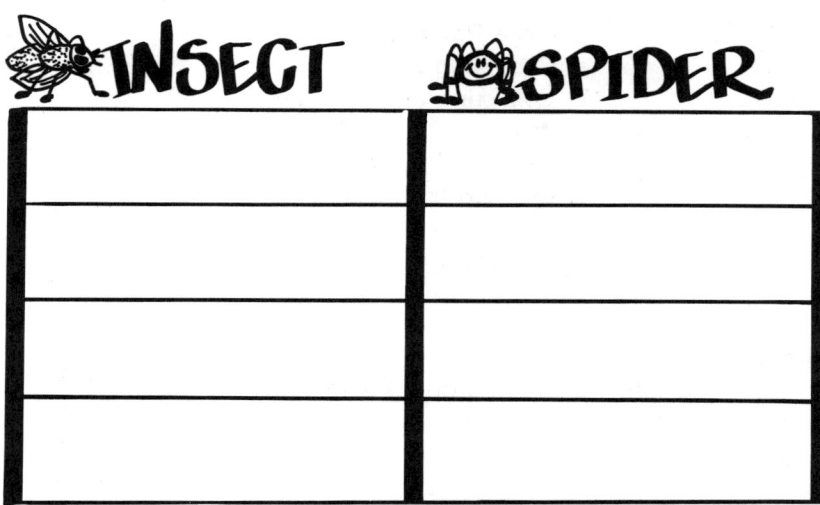

	INSECT	SPIDER
Number of legs		
Number of body parts		
Number of wings		
Number of eyes		

Observations: _____
_____

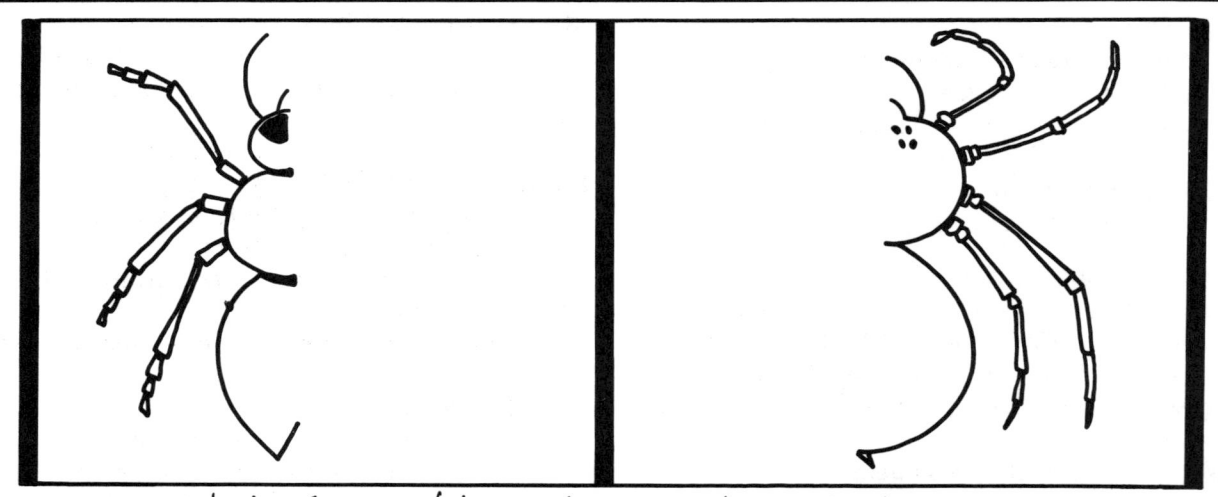

FINISH THE DRAWINGS and TELL WHAT THEY ARE

_____   _____

CRITTERS — ©1989 AIMS Education Foundation

Wings 'n Webs

Name _____

1. Make an insect or a spider out of clay, toothpicks, pipe cleaners and construction paper. Don't tell anyone what it is.

2. Draw it:

What is it? _____ Give it a name _____

3. Observe what each person in your group made:

A. I think this is a _____ because _____
   _____.

B. I think this is a _____ because _____
   _____.

C. I think this is a _____ because _____
   _____.

How many did you guess correctly? _____

CRITTERS   ©1992 AIMS Education Foundation

Wings 'n Webs

Name _____

4. Make a whole class floor graph of the insects and spiders that you made.

5. Now make your own bar graph from the floor graph.

Praying Mantis

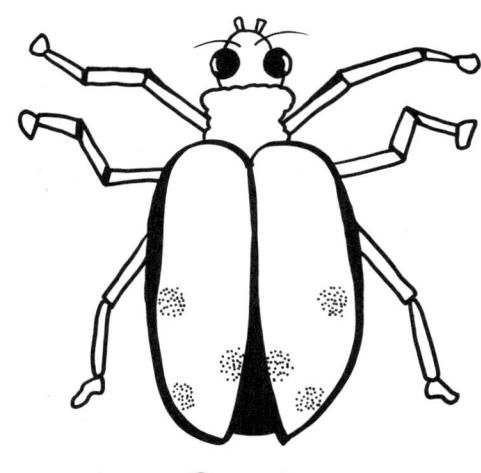
Tiger Beetle

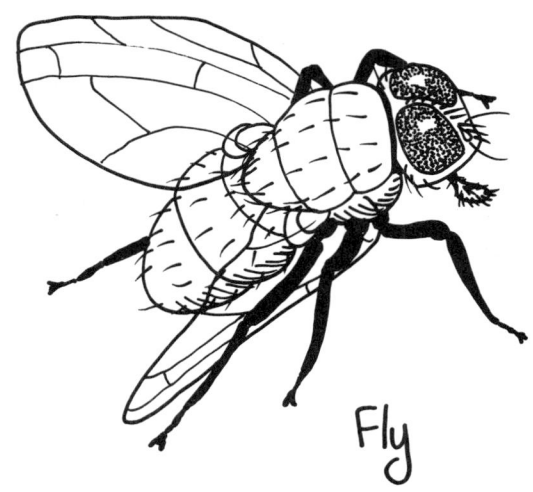
Fly

Potter Wasp

cricket

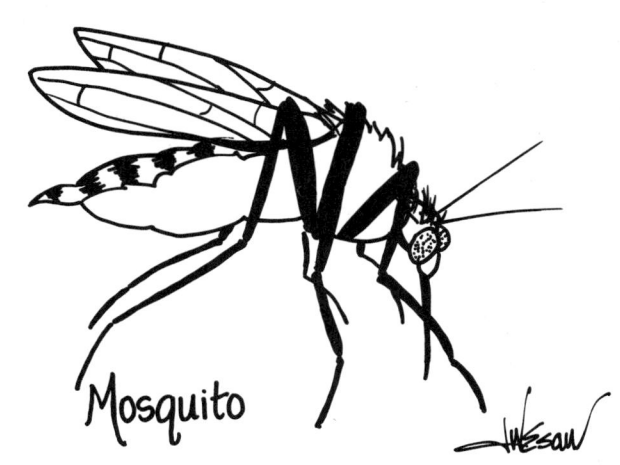
Mosquito

Black Widow Spider

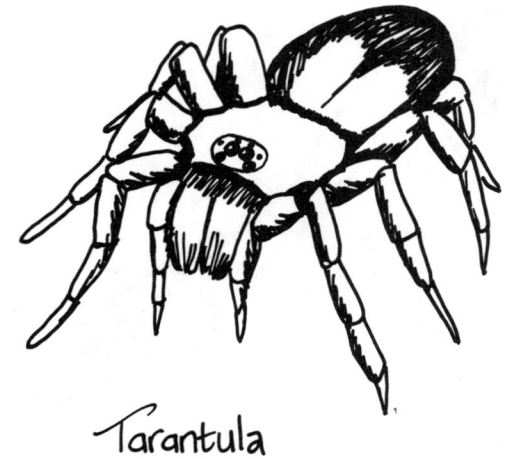
Tarantula

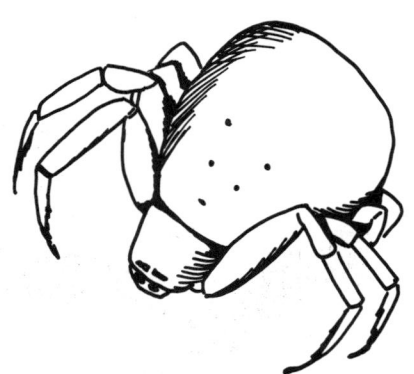
Crab Spider

Jumping Spider

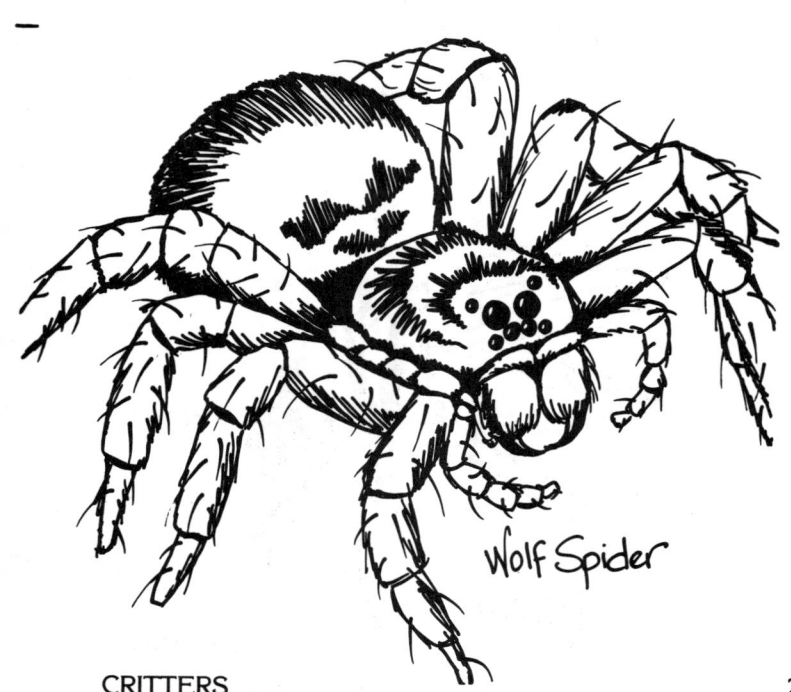
Wolf Spider

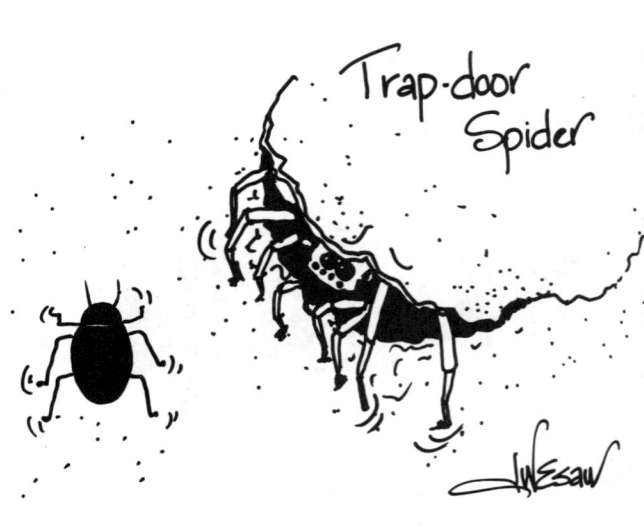
Trap-door Spider

CRITTERS   24   ©1989 AIMS Education Foundation

POPPING THROUGH THE GARDEN

I. Topic Area
Spider and insect differences

II. Introductory Statement
Students will make a pop-up spider and insect, identifying the body parts of each.

III. Math Skills   **Science Processes**
a. Counting   a. Observing
                          b. Classifying

IV. Materials
"Build a Spider and Insect" page for each student (there are two versions, one for younger students with the body parts already connected and one for older students)
scissors
glue
insect and spider fact sheets from "Wings 'N Webs"
blank paper
"Moth and Butterfly" page for each student (optional for extension activity)

V. Key Question
What are the differences between a spider and an insect?

VI. Background Information
See student fact sheets in "Wings 'N Webs"

VII. Management Suggestions
1. Teacher can write in labels on spider and insect bodies if desired.
2. This is a cooperative learning lesson. Each group will need a reader and recorder.
3. Accordion folded strips are mounted on the underside of the spider and insect creating the pop-up effect. **Note:** there are more legs than needed in each pop-up.
4. **Primary Note:** A simpler spider and insect cut out page is given with the correct number of legs for each.

VIII. Procedure
1. Make a list of all the differences between spiders and insects that are known by the class on the chalkboard. Accept all statements, even incorrect ones.
2. Form cooperative learning groups. Give each team the "Wings 'N Webs" fact pages. They are to find additional information to add to the class list (1 point for each item). Recorder records the facts for the team. Check the list for errors (1 point for each error discovered).
3. Points per team are determined.
4. See discussion questions #1-2.
5. Using the information gained, and the parts page, students will make a pop-up spider and a pop-up insect, labeling each part.
   a. select and cut out parts to be used
   b. label parts
   c. glue or tape parts together
   d. cut out accordion strip — fold on lines
   e. attach one end of strip to underneath of critter
6. On blank paper, draw an environment fit for the insect and the spider, include a web for the spider.
7. The spider and insect are then mounted on the environment page by attaching the accordion strip to the paper.

IX. Discussion Questions
1. What differences can be added to our list?
2. Why are spiders and insects in the same animal classification group? (They have segmented bodies.)
3. What parts did you have to pick in order to build the spider and to build the insects?

X. Extended Activities
1. Discuss the differences between butterflies and moths. Make a pop-up butterfly and moth.
   a. Wings — A butterfly's wings are held upright at rest; a moth folds its wings down against its body or holds them straight out to the sides.
   b. Antennae — A butterfly has knobs at the end; a moth has feathery antennae.
   c. Body — A butterfly's body is pinched in the middle and slender; a moth's body is shorter and plump.
2. Study the life cycle of butterflies or moths by actual observation. This metamorphosis can be recorded by using the "Metamorphosis Wheel" from the mealworm lessons. Students can draw each stage of the metamorphosis by observing the class collection of butterflies or moths.
3. Make a bulletin board to house all your insects and spiders.
4. Make additional insects using optional parts.

XI. Curriculum Coordinates
Language:
Write a descriptive story about your spider or insect.
Research/Art:
Find our how insects and spiders camouflage themselves and color your insect or spider accordingly.
Art:
Using yarn and popsicle sticks (or branches) — weave a web.

CRITTERS   ©1989 AIMS Education Foundation

BUILD A SPIDER AND AN INSECT

CRITTERS 26 ©1989 AIMS Education Foundation

BUILD A SPIDER AND AN INSECT

CRITTERS 27 ©1989 AIMS Education Foundation

Build a Butterfly and a Moth

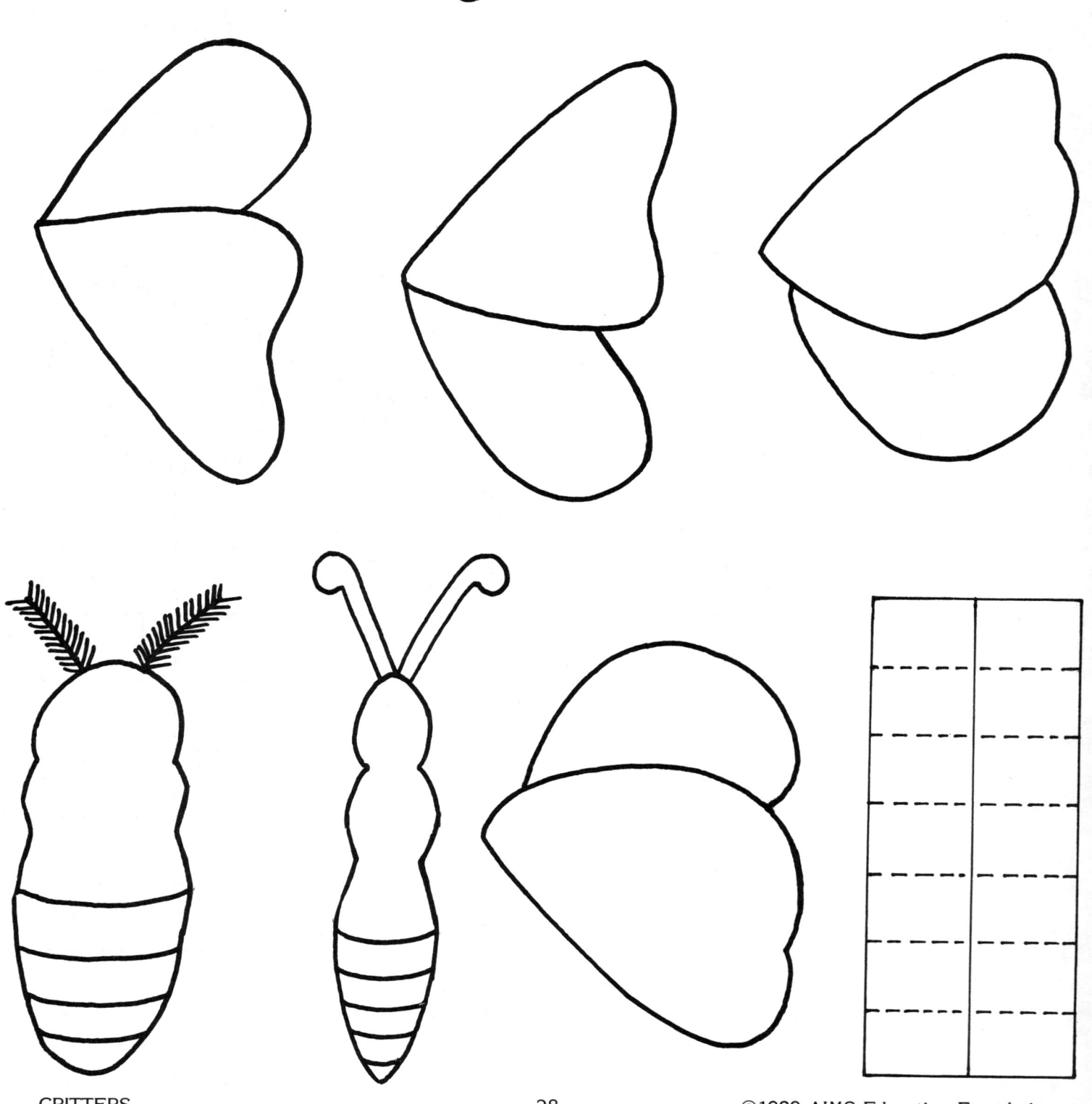

CRITTERS   28   ©1989 AIMS Education Foundation

MEALWORMS

Many insects go through four stages of growth. The changes that occur in their life cycle are called metamorphoses. Metamorphosis is a Greek word that means to transform or change. In complete metamorphosis the insect goes through four stages.

egg   larva   pupa   adult

Mealworms are the larval stage of grain beetles. The life cycle begins with white oval shaped eggs that are about 1 mm long. The eggs usually hatch in about one week. After hatching, the larvae (mealworms) begin to eat. They eat grains and soon become too large for their hard skin. The larval stage lasts for 2 to 3 weeks. The mealworm sheds its skin several times before it begins the pupa stage. Shedding its skin is called molting.

Don't bother me; I'm molting!

The pupal stage lasts for about 1 to 3 weeks. While in the pupal stage the larva transforms into the adult beetle.

I hope this is a change for the better!

MEALWORMS

When the adult comes out of the pupa case it is white. It gradually turns brown and finally black. The adult has wings but cannot fly. It can hop about 10-12 cm. The adult beetle lives only a few months. The female may lay up to 500 eggs before it dies, and the life cycle starts all over again.

Mealworms are usually found in dark damp places. They are scavengers who like to eat rotting grain and cereal. They will eat grain, cereal, flour, bran, bread, crackers, meat scraps, feathers and the bodies of dead insects.

MY MEALWORM

I. **Topic Area**
   Mealworms

II. **Introductory Statement**
   Students will use science process skills to become familiar with mealworms and their life cycles.

III. **Math Skills**
   a. Measurement

   Science Processes
   a. Observation
   b. Classification
   c. Manipulating variables
   d. Inferences

IV. **Materials**
   mealworms
   plastic shoebox or other container for classroom mealworm home
   cereal or grain
   "My Mealworm" booklet for each student

V. **Key Question**
   What do you know about mealworms?

VI. **Background Information**
   See the mealworm fact pages.

VII. **Management Suggestions**
   1. Get a supply of mealworms for your classroom from a pet store and put them in a container with some damp cereal in it.
   2. To make the "My Mealworm" booklet, collate the three activity pages, fold in half, and staple along the fold.
   3. This can be a multiple lesson activity.
   4. Allow students to familiarize themselves with their mealworm before beginning the lesson.
   5. Students can keep their mealworm at their desk in a small plastic container (cottage cheese, yogurt, etc.) with holes in the lid. Some damp cereal inside will provide food and cover for the mealworm.

VIII. **Procedure**
   1. All students receive a mealworm and a copy of the "My Mealworm" booklet.
   2. Students draw a picture of their mealworm on the cover of the "My Mealworm" booklet and give it a name.
   3. Students observe their mealworms using as many senses as possible and record their observations on the observation page.
   4. Students measure their mealworm and compare its length to other things that are longer or shorter. Record this data on "Mealworms Measure Up" page using words and/or pictures.
   5. On the center pages, which are blank, students can write and/or illustrate a story about their mealworm. Suggested topics are: "A day in the life of my mealworm", "If my mealworm could talk", poems about mealworms.
   6. Read and discuss "Mealworms on Stage" fact page.
   7. Students draw and label the four stages of the life cycle on the opposite blank page.
   8. Observe all mealworms in the classroom mealworm container and classify them as larvae, pupae or adults. Count the numbers of each and record this information on the classification chart in the booklet. This can be repeated every two weeks and the data can be compared and analyzed. Note: This activity may be postponed until after the life cycle has progressed (several weeks).
   9. On the blank page have the students draw a natural environment for mealworms.
   10. Perform the three tests on the "Watch Your Mealworm" page. Record your observations.

IX. **Discussion Questions**
   1. Are mealworms worms?
   2. Are all mealworms alike?
   3. How are your mealworms alike?
   4. How are they different?
   5. What affects a mealworm's behavior?
   6. What does a mealworm eat?

X. **Extended Activities**
   1. Find the longest mealworm in the class.
   2. Add additional pages to the booklet with comparisons, graphs, etc. on observations and measurements made.
   3. Put some food on one side of a container and your mealworm on the other side and find out how long it takes to find the food.

XI. **Curriculum Coordinates**
   Language Arts:
   Continue creative writing and poetry on the mealworm and its life cycle.

   Art:
   Design a luxury home for your mealworm.

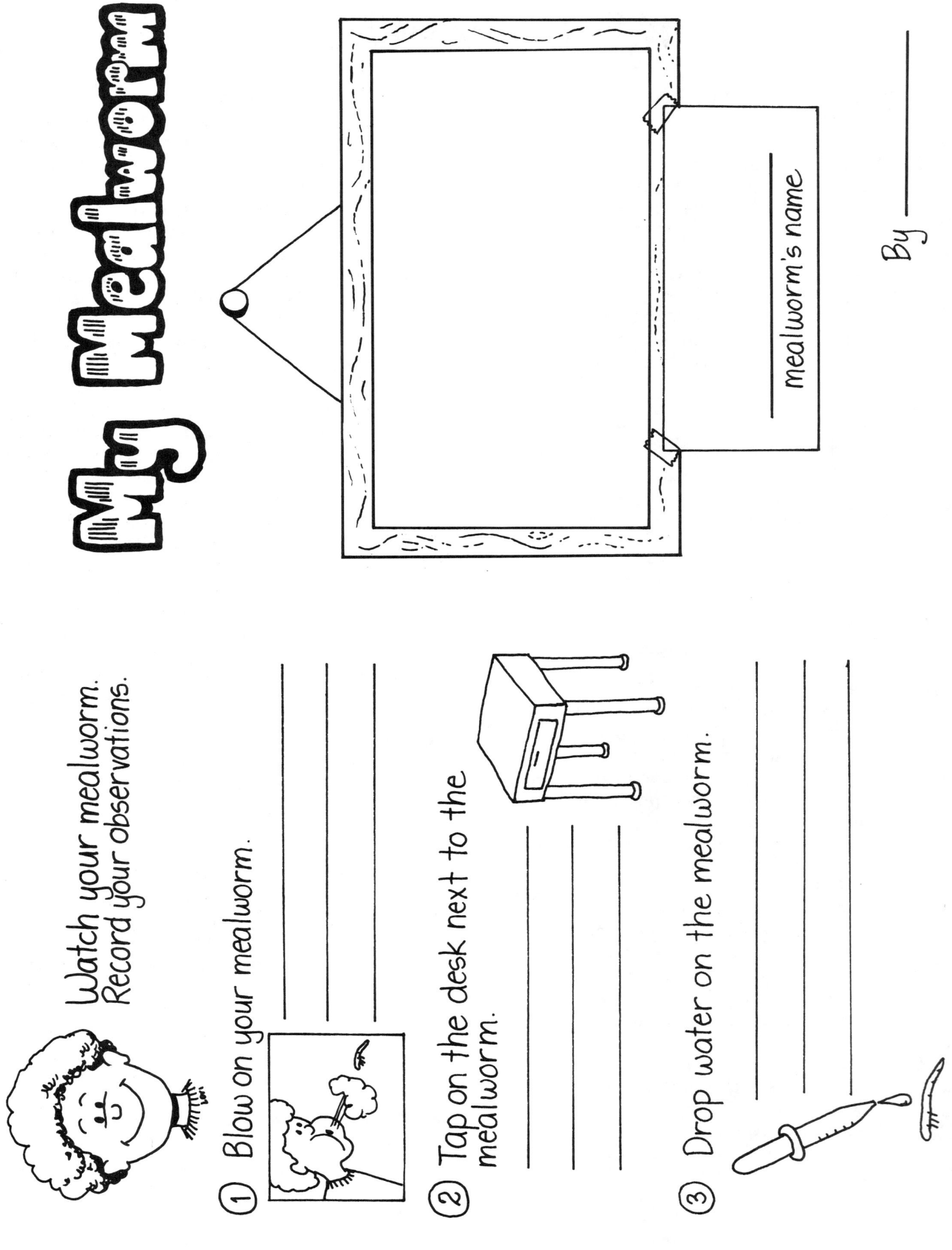

Did you ever see a mealworm go this way and that way.... go this way and that?

Observe your mealworm *carefully!*

Observation:	Sense used:				
1.					
2.					
3.					
4.					
5.					

Which sense did you use most? _____

Now, use other senses...

Observation:	Sense used:				
1.					
2.					
3.					

Classify all the mealworms in the container.

	larvae	pupae	adults
week 1			
week 3			
week 5			
week 7			

Draw a natural environment for your mealworm.

Mealworms Measure Up!

Now that you and your mealworm are friends, it's time to measure up...

✱ My mealworm measures _____ mm.

Items longer than my mealworm	Items shorter than my mealworm

Mealworms on Stage!

Mealworms have a 4 stage life cycle. They begin as tiny eggs that we can't see. The second stage is the larva or mealworm stage. Next they begin their metamorphosis and become a sleepy pupa. Finally they become a black beetle (the adult stage).

Draw the 4 stages

MEALWORMS ON STAGE

I. Topic Area
Mealworm populations

II. Introductory Statement
Students will observe and record data for a changing population of mealworms.

III. Math Skills
a. Graphing
b. Counting

Science Processes
a. Observation
b. Classification
c. Manipulating variables
d. Inferences

IV. Materials
class culture of mealworms
both "Mealworms on Stage" activity sheets for each student
Note: Students will need four copies of the first activity sheet (for group results), one for each week

V. Key Question
How will a mealworm population change over a period of four weeks?

VI. Background Information
See the mealworm fact pages.
To make a classroom culture you will need mealworms, oatmeal or bran, a plastic container and a potato. Add the bran or oatmeal to the container to form a layer two to three inches deep. Put in a supply of mealworms and both halves of a potato. A cover is not necessary.

VII. Management Suggestions
1. Buy some mealworms from a pet store and begin a class culture about two weeks before you collect the first data.
2. Make a large copy of the data table and post it on a wall above the mealworm culture.
3. Decide what day of the week you will do your population counts.
4. Make sure that students know how to identify each stage of the mealworm's life cycle.
5. Allow time for the students to observe the mealworms before beginning the population count.

VIII. Procedure
1. Each group scoops up a portion of the mealworm population to count. Make sure that all the mealworms are taken from the class culture.
2. Each group will classify their sample according to life stages and count the number of mealworms at each stage. This information will be recorded on the first page (group results page).
3. Each group will report their data and all students will fill in the data in the appropriate space on the first page.
4. After each group has reported the numbers of mealworms at each stage, students should add the columns to find the total number of mealworms in the class culture at each stage.
5. The class totals should then be recorded on the second activity sheet and the line graph begun.
6. This activity will be repeated three more times at week intervals. Each time students will need a new copy of the first activity sheet to find the group and class totals. The second activity page should be continued each week. At the end of four weeks the chart and graph will be complete.

IX. Discussion Questions
1. How many mealworms were at each stage in the life cycle?
2. How did these numbers change from the previous observation?
3. Are there any patterns in the mealworm's life cycle that can be determined from this activity?
4. Can you determine the length of each stage in the mealworm's life cycle?

X. Extended Activities
1. Continue the activity for longer than four weeks and see if any long term patterns in the mealworm's life cycle emerge.
2. Find the mass of the potato each week and explain the changes.
3. Devise a way to accurately determine the length of each stage in the mealworm's life cycle.
4. Make the "Metamorphosis Wheel" depicting the mealworm's life cycle.

XI. Curriculum Coordinates
Language Arts:
Pretend you are in the pupae stage and tell what it is like to go through metamorphosis.

Math:
Convert the numbers on the chart to percentages.

Science:
Make a list of other insects that go through a complete metamorphosis.

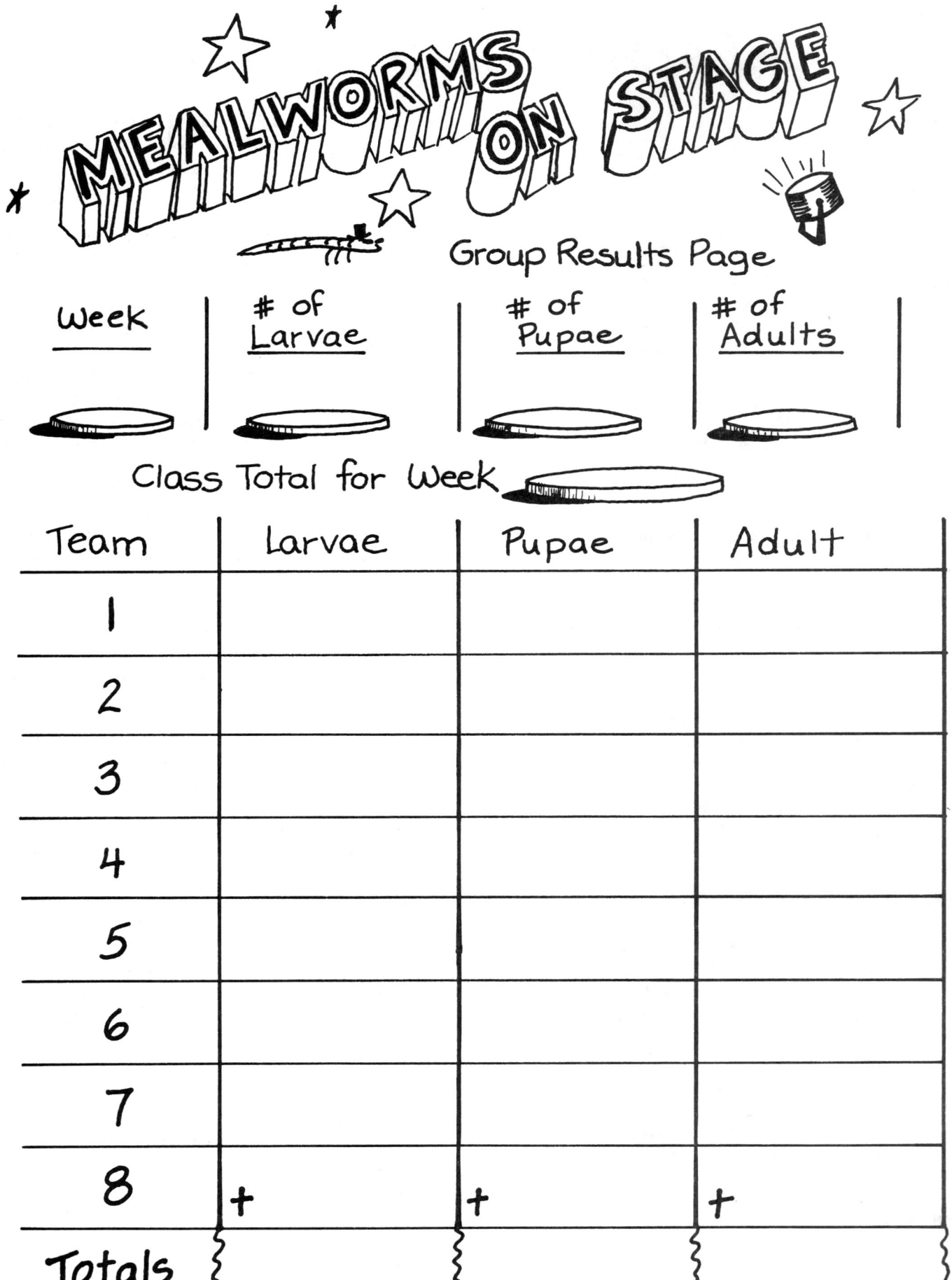

Record your mealworm population each week.

Week	Larvae	Pupae	Adult
1			
2			
3			
4			

① Complete the color key
② Make a line graph for each week

Key
☐ larvae
☐ Pupae
☐ Adult

Week 1   Week 2   Week 3   Week 4

CRITTERS 37 ©1989 AIMS Education Foundation

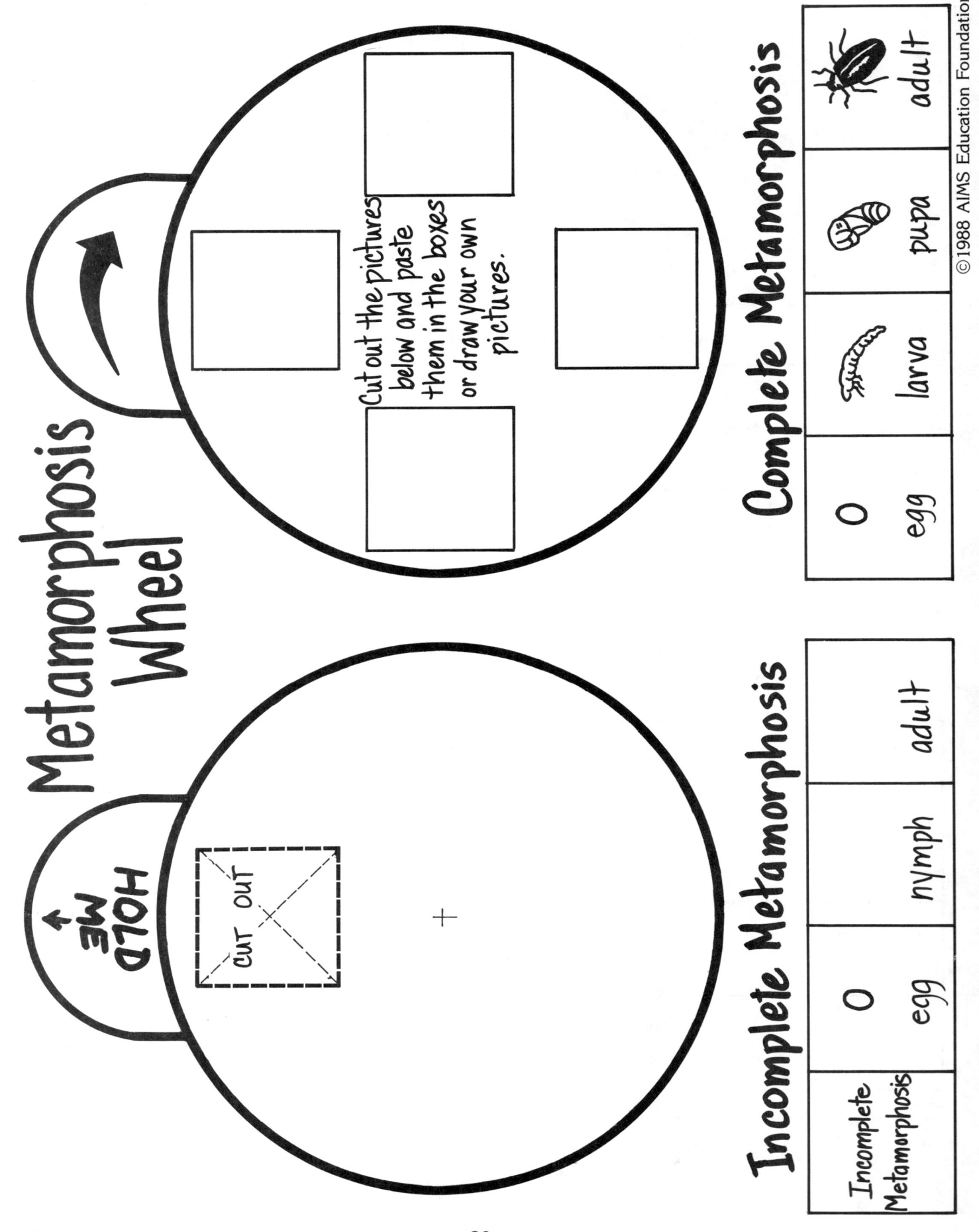

Warming Up to Worms

Topic Area
Biological Science - Earthworms

Introductory Statement
Students will observe earthworms and record their observations.

Math Skills
Predicting
Measuring
Comparing

Science
Observing
Comparing
Collecting data
Recording data

Materials
earthworms (2-4 per group)
paper towels
magnifying glasses
measuring tapes, rulers

Key Question
What can we observe about the way earthworms look and behave?

Background Information
The main sense organ of worms is their skin. A worm's skin is very sensitive to moisture, temperature, touch, and light. So, the worm actually uses its skin to see, feel, and detect moisture. The worm breathes by taking air out of the moist soil directly through its skin. (Since its skin is tender, it prefers a smooth environment over a rough one.) Its skin senses light consequently worms can tell when it is day or night. Worms are nocturnal and rarely come out of the ground except at night.

Management
1. Earthworms can be bought at bait shops or in the sporting goods departments of many large discount stores. They can also be found by digging in moist soil.
2. This is meant to be an initial observation time and should take about 20-30 minutes.
3. If working in learning groups, one student can gather and return necessary materials, a second can read observation questions, a third can report the group's observations, and a fourth can report on the observations and other questions from the group.
4. Each group should have two to four worms to observe.

Procedure
1. Distribute worms and observation guides to students.
2. Follow directions on observation guides.
3. Encourage groups to discuss their results.
4. As a class, share and discuss fundings.

Extensions
Formulate other questions about earthworms. Use the following steps to guide you:
1. Problem: What do you wish to find out?
2. Hypothesis: Predict what you think might happen.
3. Materials: What do you need to use?
4. Procedure: What will you do?
5. Results: What happened?
6. Conclusion: What answers did you find?
7. Theory: How does it change how you think about earthworms?

Warming Up to Worms

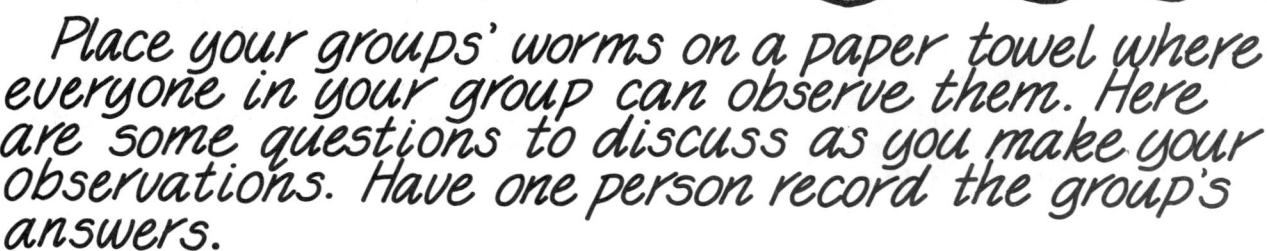

Place your groups' worms on a paper towel where everyone in your group can observe them. Here are some questions to discuss as you make your observations. Have one person record the group's answers.

1. What color are the worms?
   _____

2. What shape is an earthworm? Describe it.
   _____
   _____

3. About how long are the earthworms? How did you measure them? _____
   _____
   _____
   _____

4. How does the worm's skin feel? _____
   _____

5. Is there a difference between the top side and bottom side of a worm? If there is, describe what both are like.
   _____
   _____
   _____

CRITTERS ©1992 AIMS Education Foundation

Warming Up to Worms

6. Observe your worms with a hand lens. What do you notice that you could not see before?

_____
_____
_____

7. Answer yes or no to each of the following and tell what you observed.
   Does an earthworm have:

   Eyes? _____
   _____

   Ears? _____
   _____

   Legs? _____
   _____

   Nose? _____
   _____

   Mouth? _____
   _____

8. Can you tell which is the front end of a worm and which is its tail? Is there a difference?

_____
_____

CRITTERS ©1992 AIMS Education Foundation

Warming Up to Worms

9. Describe any other special features you notice.
   _____
   _____

10. How do worms move? Do they ever move backwards?
    _____
    _____

11. What happens when a worm meets another worm?
    _____
    _____

12. Put an obstacle in front of one of the worms? Describe its behavior.
    _____
    _____
    _____

13. Hold a worm in your hand. What does it do?
    _____
    _____
    _____

EARTHWORMS

Earthworms are often called "Nature's Plowman" because they live in the ground and tunnel their way through the ground mixing up the different layers of the soil.

WHAT DO EARTHWORMS EAT?
Earthworms eat decayed leaves and plant material. They also swallow soil and little bits of animal material.

HOW DO EARTHWORMS MOVE?
Earthworms have 2 sets of muscles:
1. <u>Circular Muscles</u> around each segment.
2. <u>Long Muscles</u> that run the length of the body.

When the circular muscles tighten, the earthworm becomes <u>longer</u> and <u>thinner</u>. When the <u>lengthwise</u> muscles tighten, the earthworm becomes <u>shorter</u> & <u>fatter</u>.

HOW DO EARTHWORMS HELP THE SOIL?
1. They mix up the different layers of the soil.
2. They add nutrients to the soil by depositing their waste products or "castings" into the soil.
3. They help to decompose dead plant and animal material into simpler parts that can be used again by new organisms.

Lumbricus terrestris

The earthworm is an invertebrate which has a segmented body. The number of segments in a full-grown earthworm varies between 120 and 175. All segments, except the first which contains the mouth and the most posterior which contains the anus, are similar. The external surfaces of segments 31 to 37 are glandular and swollen. This region is called the clitellum. This is located about one third toward the front end of the worm. This clitellum means that the worm is an adult and can mate and lay eggs.

Earthworms have regenerative powers and are capable of replacing damaged or destroyed segments depending on the region.

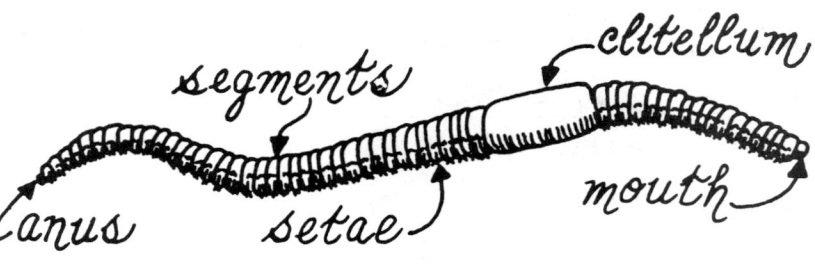

Earthworms have to stay moist in order to breathe. They have no lungs, but take oxygen from the air right through their damp skin into the blood vessels. Carbon dioxide moves out of the body the same way. Getting dried out is fatal for an earthworm.

There are bristles on the underside of the worm called setae. There are four pair on all but the first and last segments. The bristles are made of chitin which is the same material the hard outer covering of insects is composed of. These structures help the worm dig into the soil when it moves and help cling to the sides of the burrow when predators try to pull them out.

Earthworms do have enemies even though they spend much of their time underground. Their predators include birds, frogs, centipedes, moles, and man. A protective adaptation is the worm's brownish color. This makes the worm harder to see against the soil.

When observing the movement of the earthworm, you'll notice that one part of the worm stretches out, while another part squeezes together. This is because beneath the epidermis is a layer of circular muscle whose contraction decreases the diameter but increases the length of the body. Another muscle layer runs the length of the worm: the longitudinal muscle.

The earthworm has five pair of enlarged tubes which act as hearts. The tubes pump blood through the vessels of the earthworm's body.

As a worm eats enormous quantities of soil, it takes the decaying organic matter (parts of dead plants and animals) for its nourishment. From the pharynx, the food passes into the esophagus. There are several pairs of calciferous glands which secrete calcium carbonate into the esophagus. They function in the neutralization of acid soil as well as the elimination of excess carbonate from the blood.

From the esophagus, the food moves to the crop. The crop serves as a temporary storage place. From here, it passes on to the gizzard. Grains of sand are present here and the thick, muscular walls work the food and sand back and forth until the food is ground up.

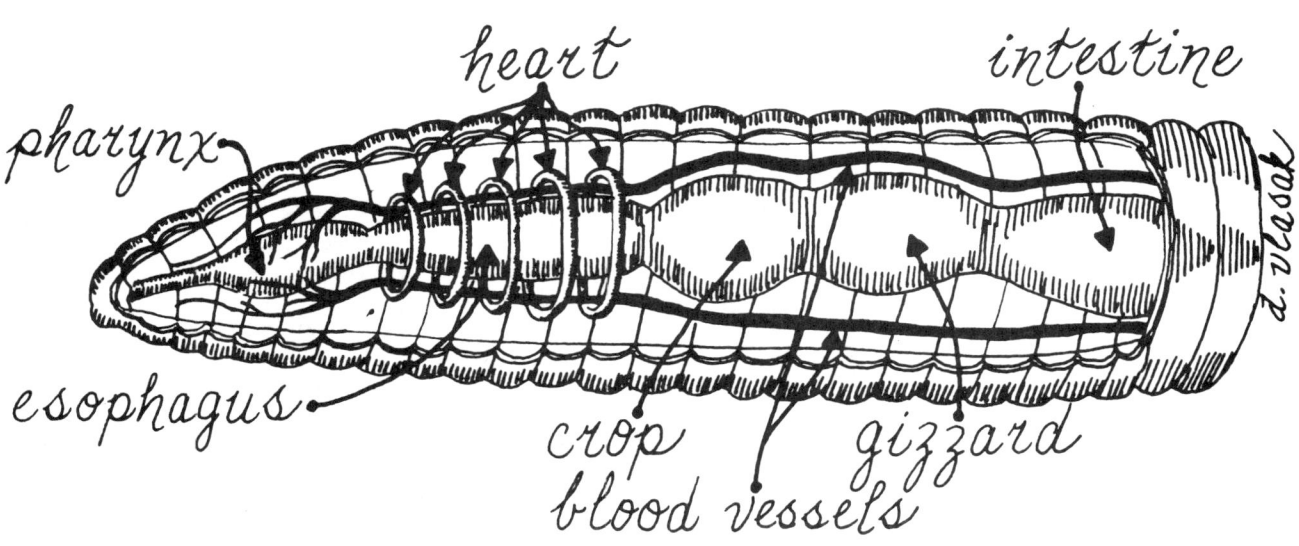

The food is then forced into the intestine, the longest section of the digestive system. The glands here secrete digestive chemicals that complete digestion and the digested food passes through the walls of the intestine and into the bloodstream. The bloodstream circulates the digested foods to other parts of the organism.

Although the earthworm is sensitive to light and touch, it does not have sense organs. There are light-sensitive cells scattered through the skin. These cells enable the worm to distinguish between light and dark. The worm is also sensitive to vibrations which is a useful adaptation since it's the mole's favorite food.

Boy or girl? The earthworm is actually both. It is called a hermaphrodite because it has both ovaries and testes. The two pairs of testes are located in segments 10 and 11, counting from the anterior end, and the pair of ovaries are in segment 13. Self-fertilization cannot take place. The exchange of sperm cells between two mating worms occurs during a process called copulation. Copulation usually occurs at night during moist weather and involves a temporary union of two individuals along their ventral surfaces. A worm is old enough to lay eggs at about one year.

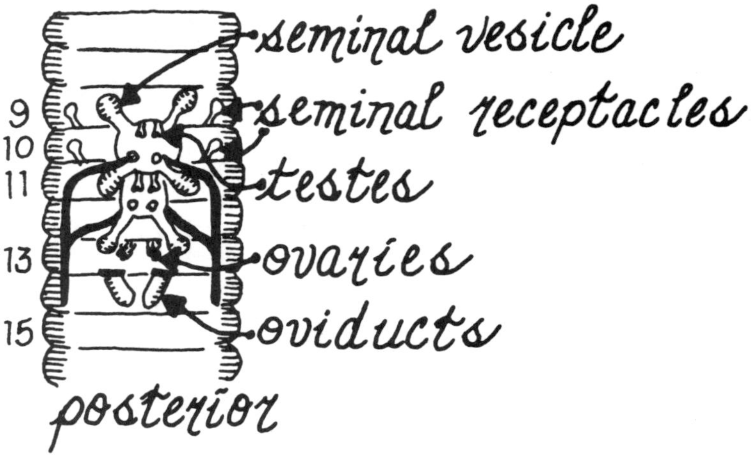

anterior
- seminal vesicle
- seminal receptacles
- testes
- ovaries
- oviducts

posterior

After copulation, the worms separate, each having the other's sperm stored in the seminal receptacles until used for fertilization.

When the eggs have reached maturity and have been released, the clitellum secretes a tube of mucus which slips over the front of the worm. The tube receives eggs as it passes segment 14, and receives the other worm's sperm cells as it passes segments 9 and 10. Fertilization occurs inside the tube as it slides forward until it finally slips off the anterior end. The tube, which is then sealed, is usually left in the burrow to form a cocoon containing several zygotes. After three to four weeks, pale, whitish wormlets crawl out as miniature adults. If the moisture and temperature are not quite right, the eggs can stay in the case for a year or more.

Because the earthworm's source of nutrition is organic matter in the soil, large

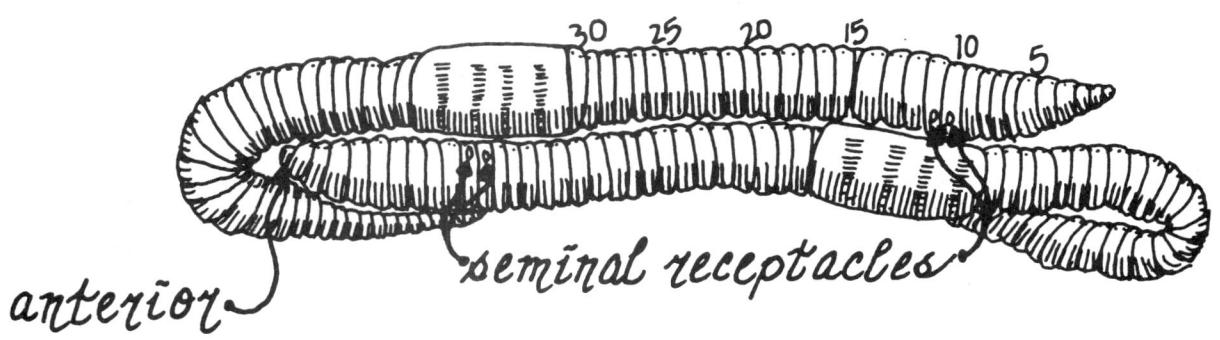

30
25
20
15
10
5
seminal receptacles
anterior

quantities of soil are eaten. The undigestible soil passes through their intestinal tract and is eliminated as "worm castings". This helps enrich the soil. Lower levels of earth are brought to the surface which improves the chemical composition. In burrowing, they are also improving farm land as air and water can enter the ground easier. The naturalist Charles Darwin once calculated that an acre of farm land may contain as many as 50,000 earthworms. In the course of a year, those worms could overturn as much as eighteen tons of soil per acre! This is of great significance to agriculture and these creatures should be appreciated for their contribution to farming.

d. vlasak

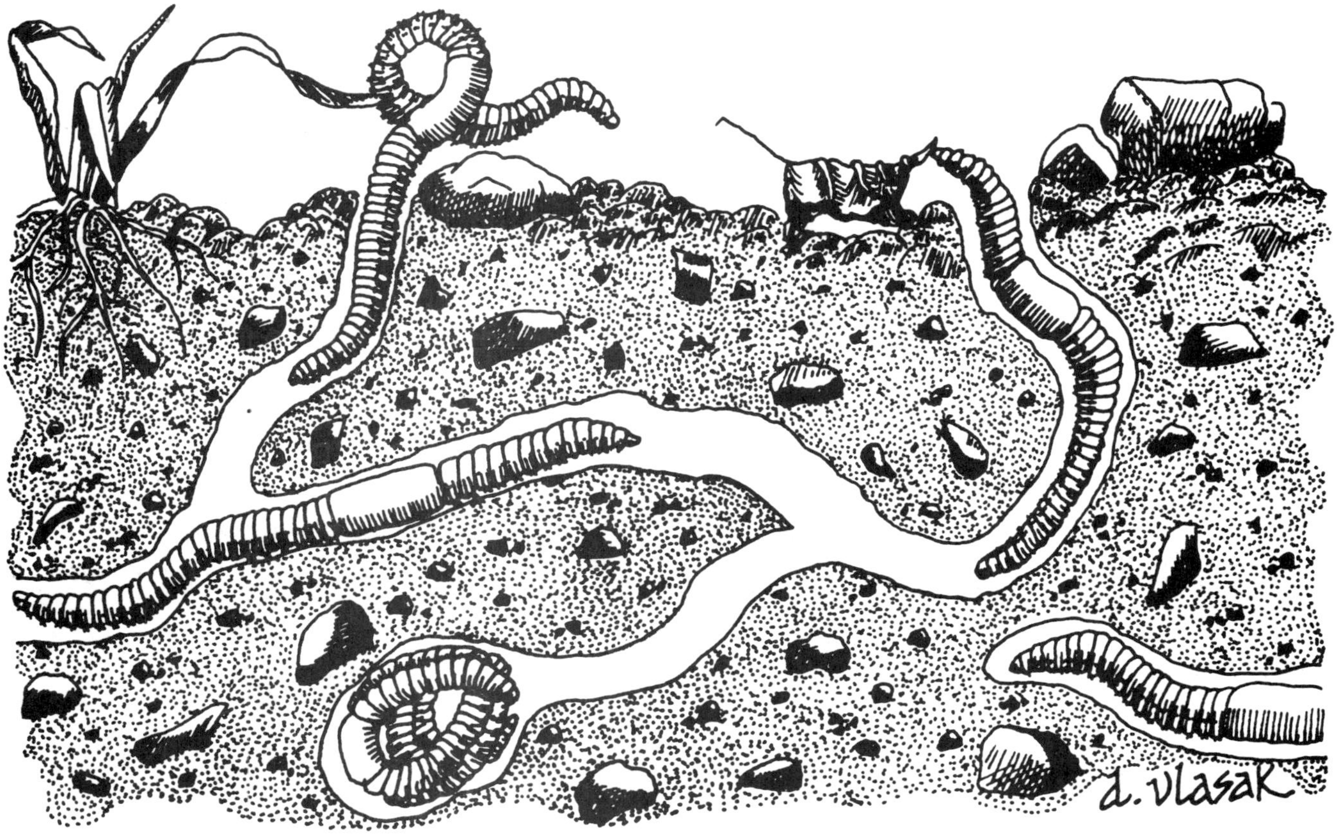

FAVORITE FOODS

Based on scientists' observations of feeding habits, these seem to be favorites among worms

Fresh Leaves — order of preference:
- beech
- maple
- oak
- horse chestnut
- lime
- willow

Decaying Leaves — order of preference:
- willow
- oak
- lime
- beech
- maple
- horse chestnut

Set up your own experiment to find your worm's preference.

You can also feed your worms fruit peelings, corn meal, and bread crumbs. Two tablespoonsful every other week should be enough. Do not feed them too much or the food may spoil.

EXTERNAL STRUCTURES

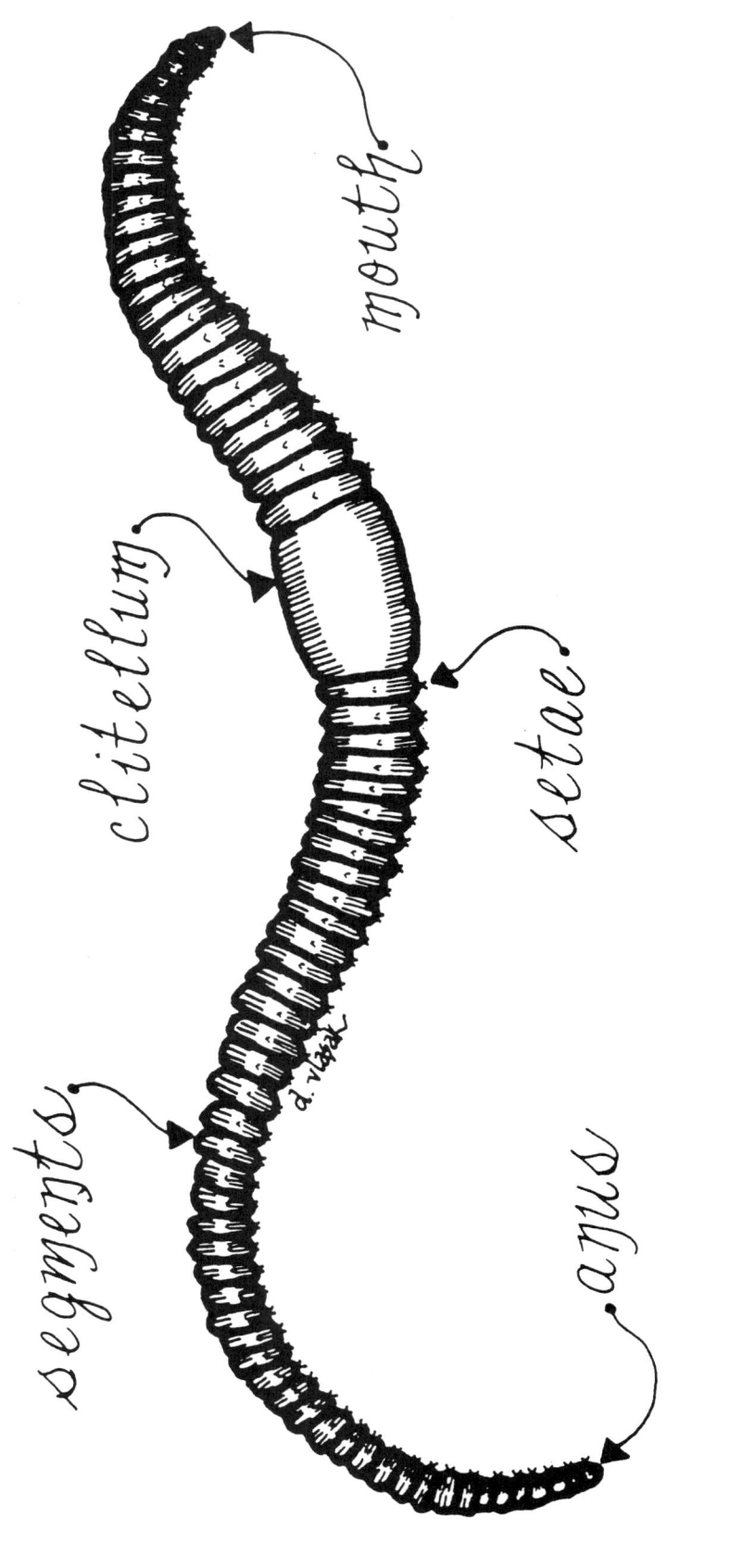

PHYLUM ANNELIDA

CRITTERS ©1992 AIMS Education Foundation

ORGANS AND FUNCTIONS

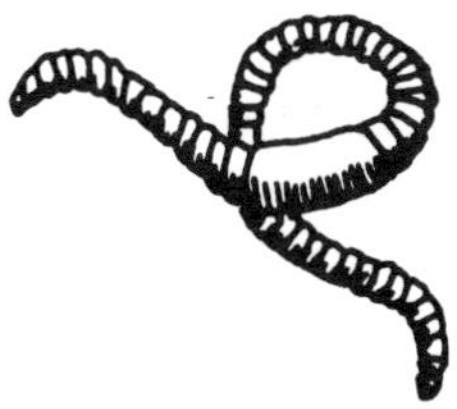

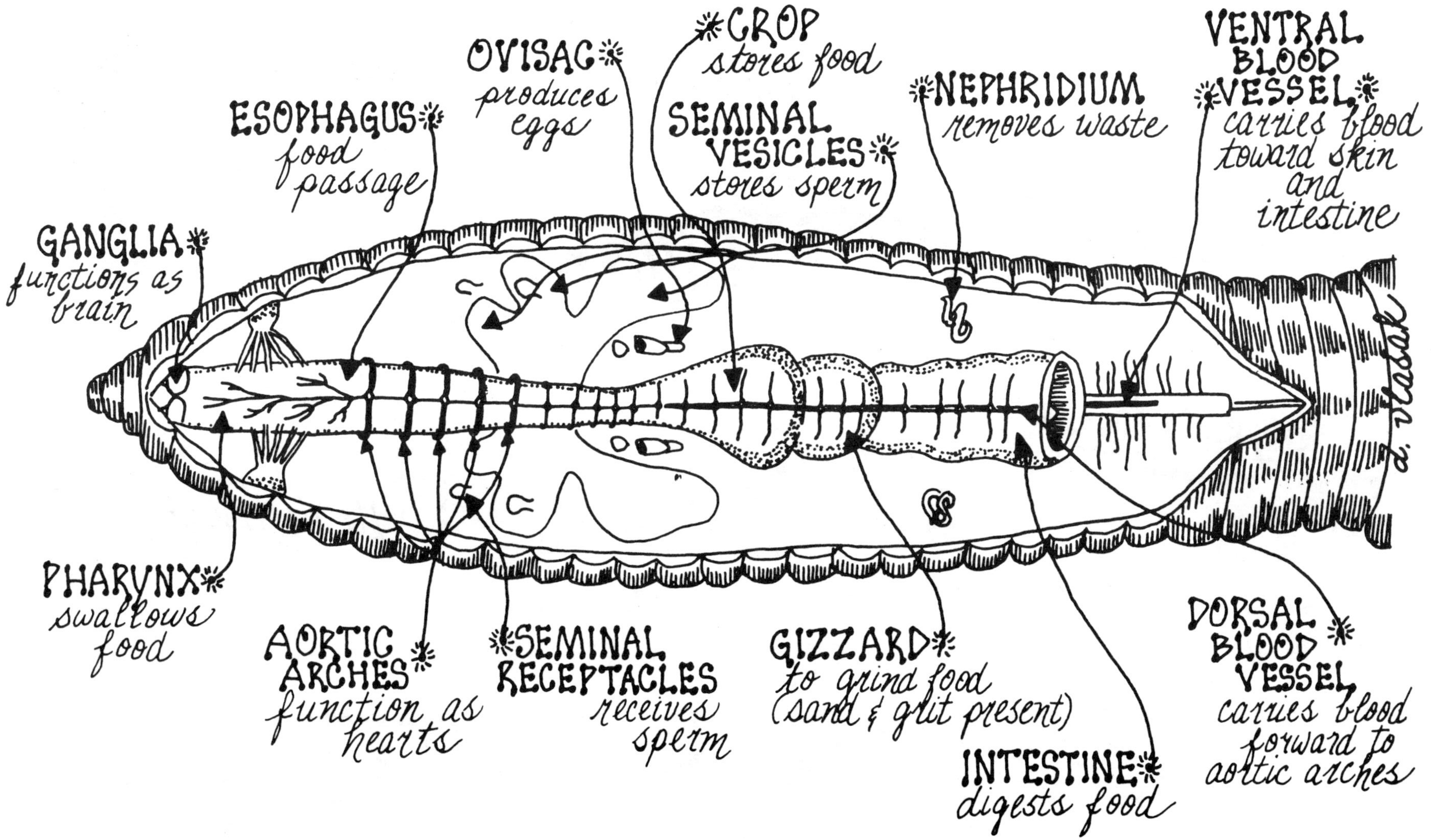

VENTRAL BLOOD VESSEL — carries blood toward skin and intestine

NEPHRIDIUM — removes waste

CROP — stores food

SEMINAL VESICLES — stores sperm

OVISAC — produces eggs

ESOPHAGUS — food passage

GANGLIA — functions as brain

PHARYNX — swallows food

AORTIC ARCHES — function as hearts

SEMINAL RECEPTACLES — receives sperm

GIZZARD — to grind food (sand & grit present)

INTESTINE — digests food

DORSAL BLOOD VESSEL — carries blood forward to aortic arches

CRITTERS 50 ©1992 AIMS Education Foundation

THE MUSCULAR SYSTEM

Muscle cells cause movement by contracting and relaxing. The earthworm has two layers of muscle tissue. One layer circles the worm as the circular muscle. The other layer runs the length of the worm as the longitudinal muscle.

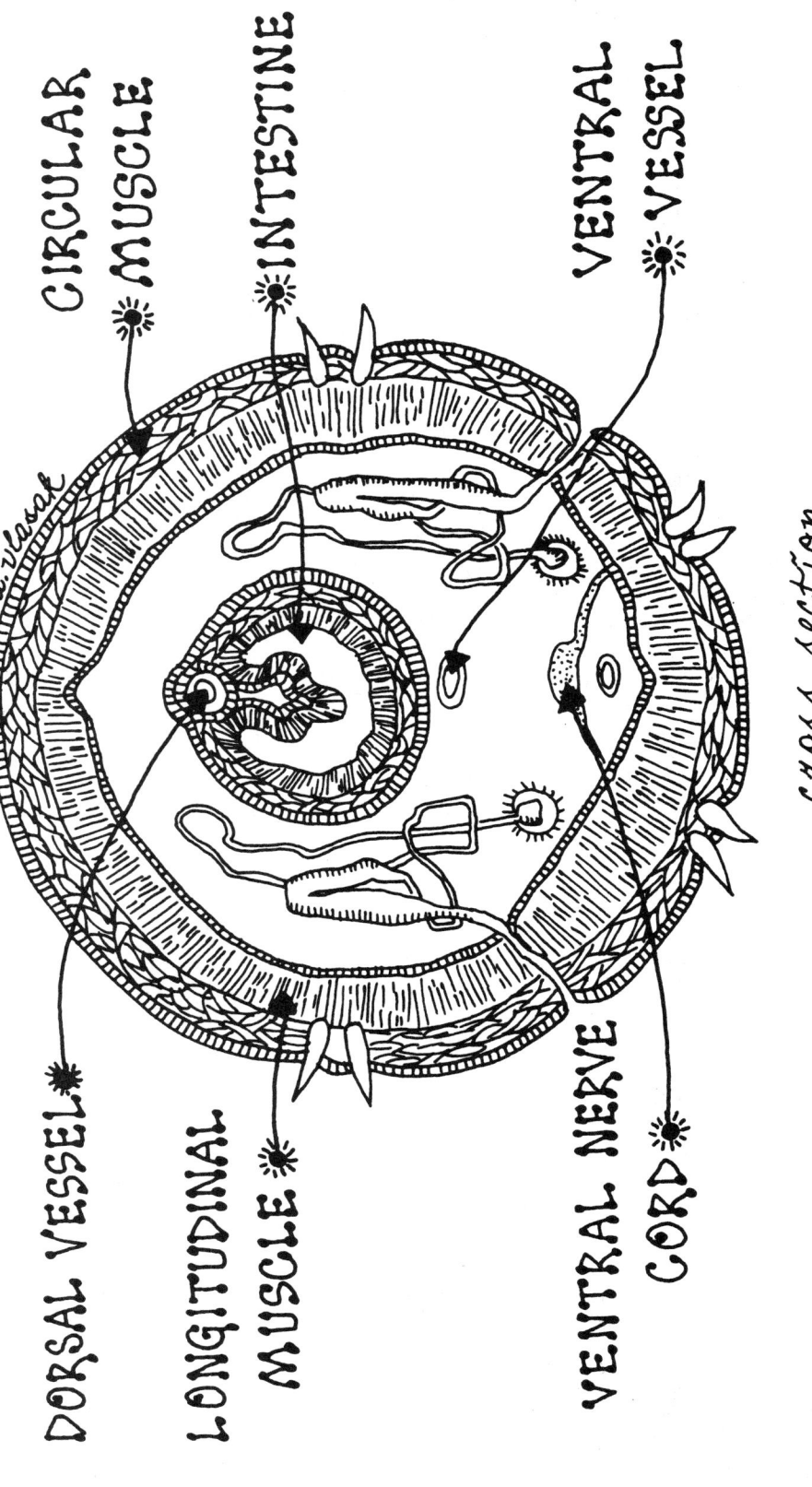

- CIRCULAR MUSCLE
- INTESTINE
- VENTRAL VESSEL
- VENTRAL NERVE CORD
- LONGITUDINAL MUSCLE
- DORSAL VESSEL

cross section

WORM HOME

You can create a temporary environment for earthworms so you can make detailed observations. A plastic container would be safest and drainage holes could be punched in the bottom. A plastic shoebox would work well. If you use a container that can't have drainage, put a layer of sand or gravel on the bottom to collect excess water.

Fill the jar three quarters full of a mixture of fine sand and good loamy soil. Hard soils are too hard and compact for the worms to burrow through. Keep the soil moist, but not soaked. One teaspoon of coffee grounds and one fourth teaspoon of brown sugar layered on top will serve as a food source. The ideal temperature should be kept about 50°F and black construction paper wrapped around the jar will provide the dark environment the worms like best.

- leaves
- coffee grounds
- topsoil and sand
- gravel

The size of your container will determine the number of worms you can keep. A one gallon jar can hold up to a dozen worms but after your observations, you should return the worms to the ground where they can make a good home.

reaction to light

Do earthworms prefer light or darkness?

Remove the lid from a shallow box and cut in half widthwise. Line the bottom of box with damp paper towels. Place five worms in each half of box and place the lid on top.

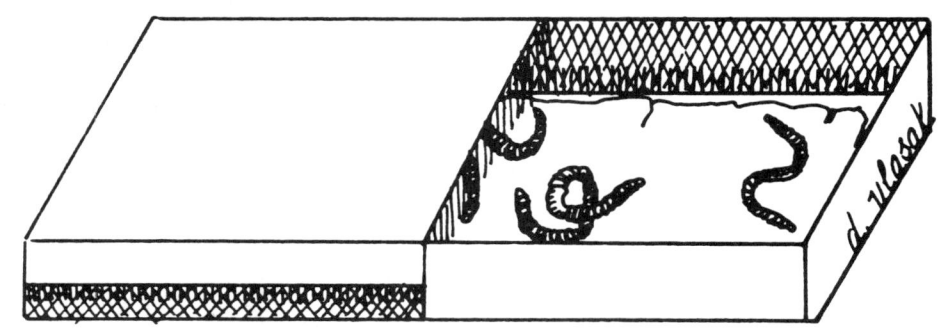

After five minutes, record the number of worms in each section.

test #	# on light area	# on dark area
1		
2		
3		
average		
ratio		
percentage		

Conclusions:

_____
_____
_____
_____
_____

reaction to touch

Do earthworms react to touch?

Remember to be very gentle with the worm for this experiment. We want to test if a worm is sensitive to touch. Put the worm on a moist paper towel. Very gently touch the worm at the posterior (rear) end and record your observations. Do the same at the middle section and the anterior (front) end. Record your observations. This should be done with several worms to see if results are consistent.

section touched	response
posterior	
middle	
clitellum	
anterior	

What are your conclusions about an earthworm's sensitivity to touch?

_____
_____
_____
_____
_____

CRITTERS

reaction to moisture

Do earthworms prefer moist or dry areas?

This test can be done using paper towels or soil. When using toweling, put two side by side: one dampened with water and the other dry. Place five worms on each side and check after five minutes to recount the number on each towel. Test this many times for accuracy and record your results.

TEST	number on dry towel	number on moist towel
1		
2		
3		

percentage of total that preferred the moist environment
%

percentage of total that preferred the dry environment
%

Your conclusion: _____
_____
_____

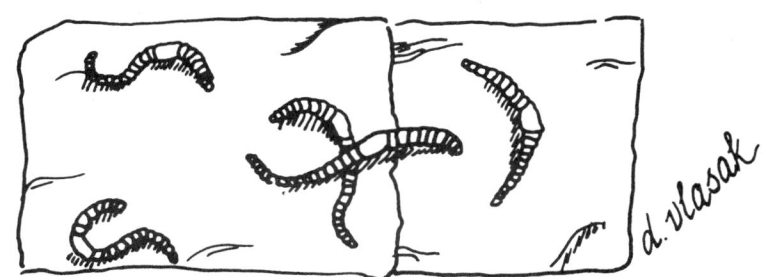

The same procedure can be done in a tray with soil. One section should be damp and the other dry.

NOW YOU SEE THEM, NOW YOU DON'T

I. **Topic Area**
   Earthworms

II. **Introductory Statement**
   Students will determine how long it takes earthworms to burrow into the ground.

III. **Math Skills**   **Science Processes**
   a. Estimating   a. Observing
   b. Measuring   b. Collecting & organizing data
   c. Graphing   c. Generalizing
   d. Problem solving   d. Hypothesizing

IV. **Materials**
   earthworms
   plastic cups of loosely packed soil
   watch or clock with a second hand
   activity sheets

V. **Key Question**
   How long will it take a worm to burrow into the ground?

VI. **Background Information**
   See worm fact sheets.

VII. **Management Suggestions**
   1. This activity is best done in small groups.
   2. Make sure you have enough worms. Each group needs three.
   3. The soil used for this activity should be moist (but not too wet) and loosely packed.
   4. The worms should be put in one at a time. The students can then make better informed estimates of the time it will take the second and third worms to dig into the soil.

VIII. **Procedure**
   1. Pass out and discuss the activity sheet.
   2. Divide the class into small groups and pass out a plastic cup to each group. The cup may already have the soil in it or it can be filled by the students.
   3. Pass out three worms to each group.
   4. Have students estimate the time they think the first worm will take to burrow into the soil and record their predictions on the activity sheet.
   5. Place the first worm in the cup and time how long it takes to completely burrow into the soil. Record that time on the activity sheet.
   6. Repeat the above process with the next two worms.
   7. Discuss the results and complete the graph.
   8. Discuss the question at the bottom of the page and have students explain how they could devise an experiment to find out.

IX. **Discussion Questions**
   1. Did all the worms take the same amount of time to burrow into the soil? Why?
   2. What would the effect of packing the soil more tightly have?
   3. What would happen if you used different types of soil?

X. **Extended Activities**
   1. Repeat the activity with three cups of the same soil, but varying compactness.
   2. Repeat the activity with various types of soil such as moist sand, sandy loam, moist potting soil, etc.

CRITTERS   ©1989 AIMS Education Foundation

Now You See Them, Now You Don't.

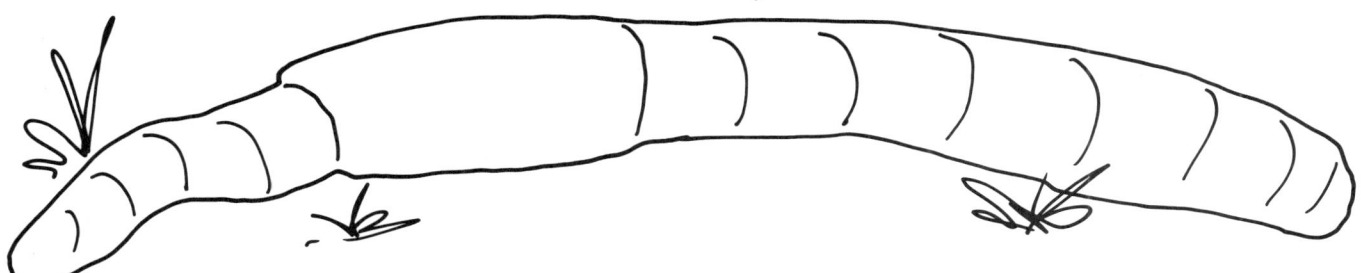

How long will it take a worm to go underground?

Type of soil:

_____

	Guess:	Actual
Worm #1		
Worm #2		
Worm #3		

Do you think different types of soil will affect the time it takes to go underground?

How could you find out?

_____
_____
_____

2 min. — 120

1 min. — 60

seconds

Worm #1	Worm #2	Worm #3

CRITTERS

Using a hand lens, observe your snail carefully. Locate the following parts:

EYES	MOUTH	RESPIRATORY PORE
OPTIC NERVE	RADULA	BODY WHORL
TENTACLES FOR FEELING	EDGE OF MANTLE	APEX OF SHELL

Sprinkle some cornmeal in front of your snail so you can observe its manner of eating. In order to see the radula in action, clear acetate can be used so as to lift the sheet and look up from beneath. How would you describe the snail's manner of eating?

_____

_____

Arrange sharp and jagged objects on a table top and place your snail in front of the obstacles. Don't worry; even a knife edge won't hurt the snail because of that layer of slime it produces to slide on.

OBJECT ←——————→ SNAIL'S REACTION ←——————→

←——————→   ←——————→

←——————→   ←——————→

Snail Observations

Place your snail on a flat surface and observe the way it travels. How would you describe its locomotion?

_____

_____

Allow the snail to stretch out next to the metric tape at the bottom of this page. Take three different readings of what you think is its full extension, and average to find the full body length of your snail.

trial 1 _____ cm   trial 2 _____ cm   trial 3 _____ cm

average _____ cm

Gently touch an optic antenna and record the result.

_____

Now touch one of the shorter antenna. What happened?

_____

height of snail
(to top of shell)

_____ cm

mass of snail

_____ g

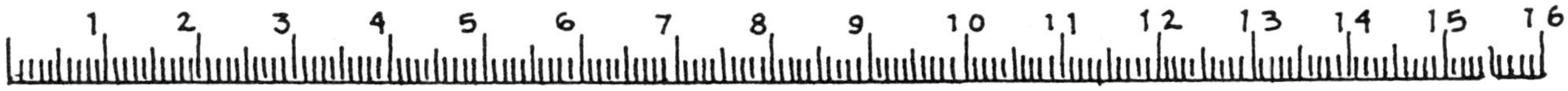

Snails

Snails are animals that are classified as invertebrates (no backbone). They have a soft body that is covered by a coiled shell. A snail's body has a head with eyes, tentacles, a mouth and tiny teeth. The snail creeps along using a strong muscular organ called a foot. It has tiny glands that make a layer of shiny slime. A snail protects its foot by sliding across the layer of slime.

Snails like to live in a moist environment. When it is too hot and dry a snail will curl up inside its shell and seal its opening with a layer of slime (mucus). Some snails can remain in their shells for two years waiting for the environment to become moist again.

Snails eat plants and rotting vegetation. They have tiny teeth which are attached to their tongues. They use this saw-like tongue to shred their food into small pieces. Snails usually feed in the late evening and at night.

Snails

Snails belong to a phylum known as mollusks. Mollusks have soft bodies and many have shells during some stage in their lives. Snails are univalves, meaning they have only one shell.

Gastropod is another scientific name for snails. It comes from the Greek word meaning "belly-foot." Snails were given this name because they seem to walk on their "belly" or "foot." It is the long, flat piece of tissue and muscle that the animal crawls on. The front end of this "foot" is the snail's head which includes a mouth, eyes, and sense organs called tentacles. Most of the snail's internal organs are within the shell.

A snail has two pair of tentacles. The eyes are located on the longer pair. A snail can distinguish lights and darks, but probably can't see clear images. The two shorter tentacles are sensitive to touch and are used to feel objects in the snail's path. Both sets of tentacles can be moved in all directions and pulled within the shell if the snail becomes frightened.

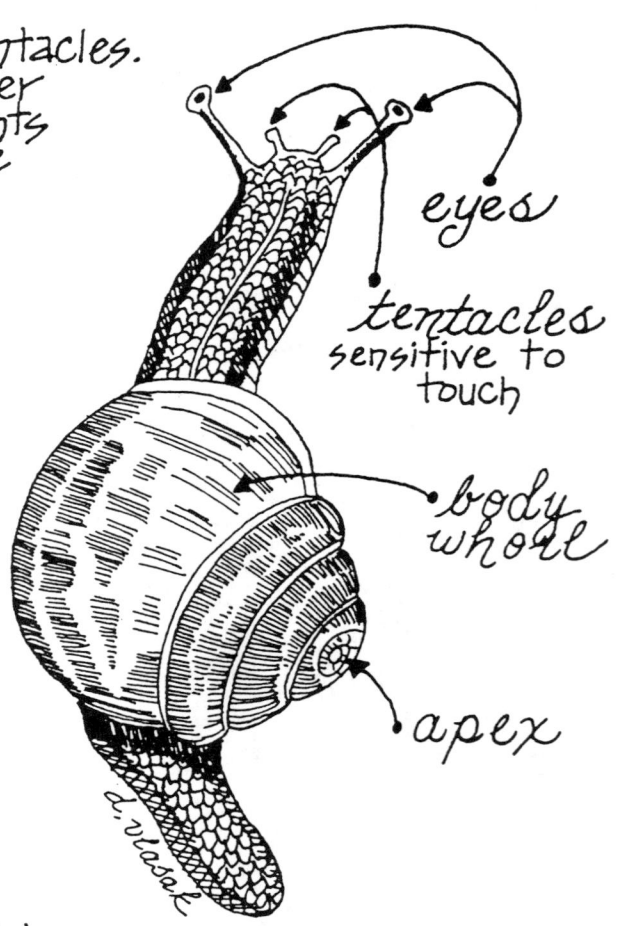

A snail's mouth is on the front of the head and inside is an organ called the radula. It is a long, flat tongue covered with rows of tiny, sharp teeth. When a snail eats, it moves the radula back and forth like a file in order to scrape off pieces of food.

After food passes through the digestive tract, waste material leaves the snail's body through the anal opening. Because of the twisting of the internal organs, this opening is at the front of the body in a space under the edge of the shell called the mantle cavity.

Next to the anal opening in the mantle cavity is a larger opening called the respiratory pore. This is where the snail takes air into its body. The pore connects to lungs which draw oxygen from the air and expel carbon dioxide.

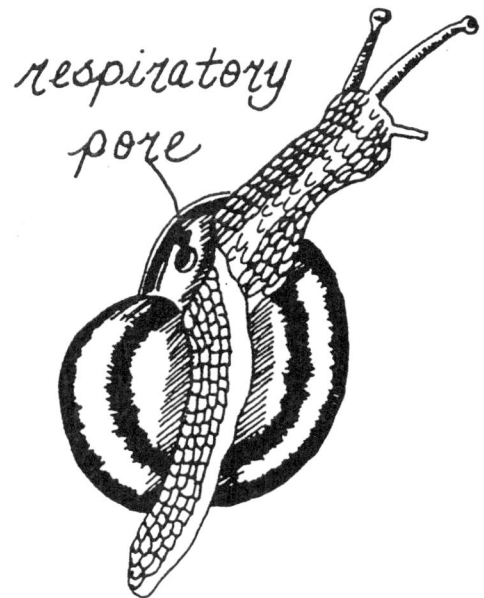
respiratory pore

A snail can glide easily on its foot because of a slippery liquid that comes from a gland at the front of the foot. This mucus protects the snail from sharp or rough textures and allows it to cling to vertical surfaces. The trail can be seen behind a passing snail.

Snails withdraw into their shells when danger is near, but even that instinct cannot protect them from some of their predators. Birds, frogs, toads, small mammals, and insects are some of their enemies. Man, of course, is another enemy as snails are considered a delicacy in many parts of the world.

A snail will also withdraw into its shell if the weather conditions aren't right. They pull within the shell to keep their moist body from drying out. The shell is sealed by a thin film of mucus that becomes dry and hard forming a tight covering. A snail may produce as many as six of these "doors" depending on the coldness with a tiny hole left open for air to enter. This state is called estivation and may last several months until conditions are favorable. In areas of cold winters, snails will seal themselves inside the shell for the entire winter so this would be hibernation.

Snails are hermaphrodites meaning they produce both male and female sex cells. It cannot reproduce by itself though, and must have another snail's sperm for fertilization. There is a courtship that takes place at the time of mating. A snail looking for a mate will slowly circle around another

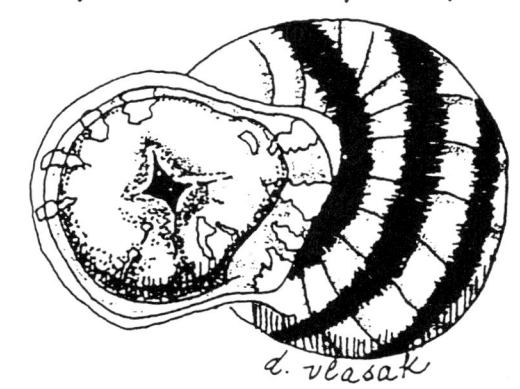
d. vlasak

snail. They may rub heads and feet together then each snail jabs its partner with a small, sharp dart. These tiny darts are made of shell-like materials and are produced in special sacs inside the snail's body. The darts may be a way for two snails to make sure they've found the right partners or get the snails' bodies ready for mating. After darting, they exchange sperm by depositing it through an opening near the head called the genital pore. Inside the body, the sperm fertilize the eggs and mating is complete.

Actual dart is about 1/5 of an inch (5mm) long

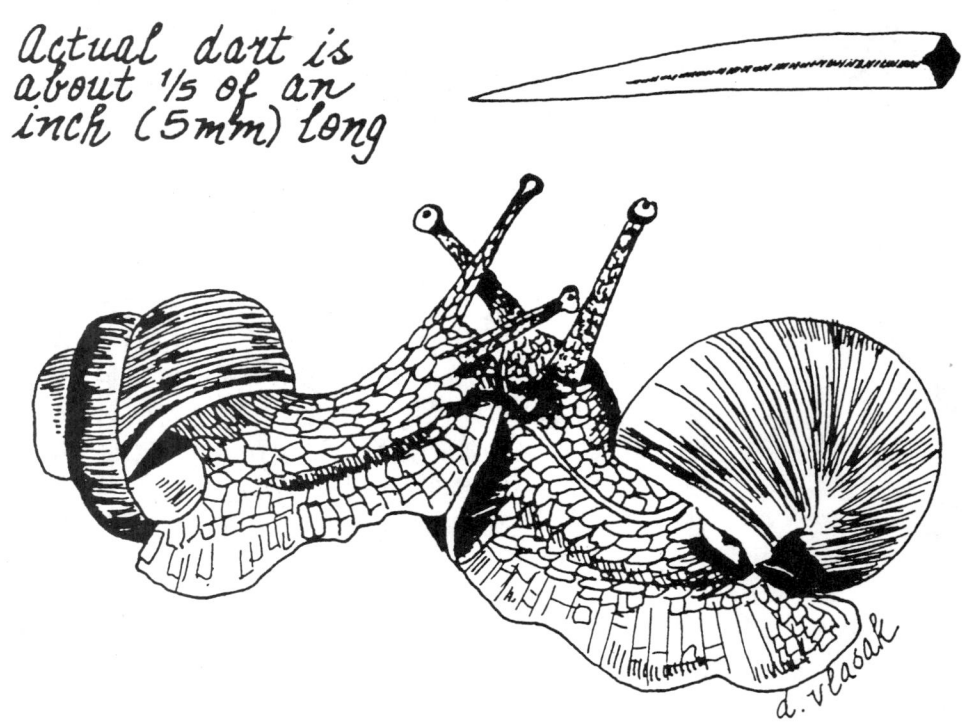

About a month later, they are both ready to lay eggs. A snail uses its head to push aside the dirt to make a hole about 10 centimeters deep or may lay its eggs under leaves, rocks, or bark of trees. The eggs come through the genital pore, each being about 3 millimeters in diameter. A snail may lay from 50 to hundreds of eggs and then leaves them to develop on their own.

Each egg has a yolk (food material) to nourish the embryo while inside the egg. After three to four weeks the new little snails crawl out looking like their parents, except their bodies and shells are smaller. The shell is soft and thin but will harden as the snail grows. It will also grow more coiled sections called whorls.

The first meal for the babies will usually be the empty eggs and then they look for green plants, especially tender shoots of young plants.

As the young snail grows, new whorls are formed in the shell. As the whorls form, the body containing the internal organs, or visceral hump, twists along with it. When this happens, the organs that were originally in back of the snail's body move toward the front. The digestive system develops a U-turn and the opening for expelling waste moves to a position near the head. Each newly formed whorl is larger than the one before and overlaps the whorl before at a slightly lower level. The highest point of a snail's shell is called the apex and is the oldest section. The newest section is the large body whorl from which the head and foot emerge.

The snail has a primitive brain, a two-chambered heart which pumps blood through its veins, a complicated digestive system, a liver, kidneys, lungs, sex organs, and a nervous system. It also has a strong columella muscle which attaches to its shell and enables the head and foot to be extended or withdrawn.

On the inside of the shell is a fleshy lining called the mantle. Glands located in the mantle secrete a limy substance which is deposited on the rim of the shell opening then hardens and becomes shell. If the shell gets a crack in it or a piece on the lip breaks off, the mantle can repair it. If the shell is badly broken, the snail will die.

Snails' food consists mainly of broad-leaved plants; like lettuce, spinach, dandelions, etc. An important part of their diet is calcium, necessary for producing its shell. Snails get calcium from stones, cement wall, etc. If you are keeping snails for observation, you can be sure they receive necessary calcium by mixing crushed limestone and flour or putting clean, white chalk or the shell of a chicken egg into their container.

As you can see, snails are interesting and complex creatures. You can now devise experiments to test reactions and behavior or set up a temporary home so as to make detailed observations.

INNER VIEW OF HEAD

1. mouth
2. horny jaw
3. radula
4. cartilage supporting radula
5. radula sac from which radula grow
6. muscle which retracts buccal mass
7. muscles that rotate the radula
8. cerebral ganglion
9. pedal & visceral ganglia
10. esophagus
11. tentacles
12. eye tentacles
13. salivary gland
14. mucus gland

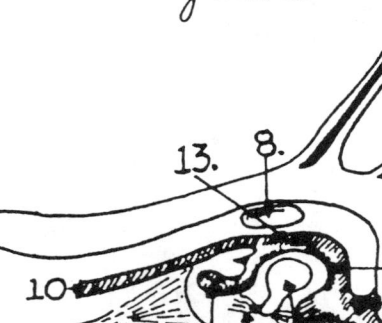

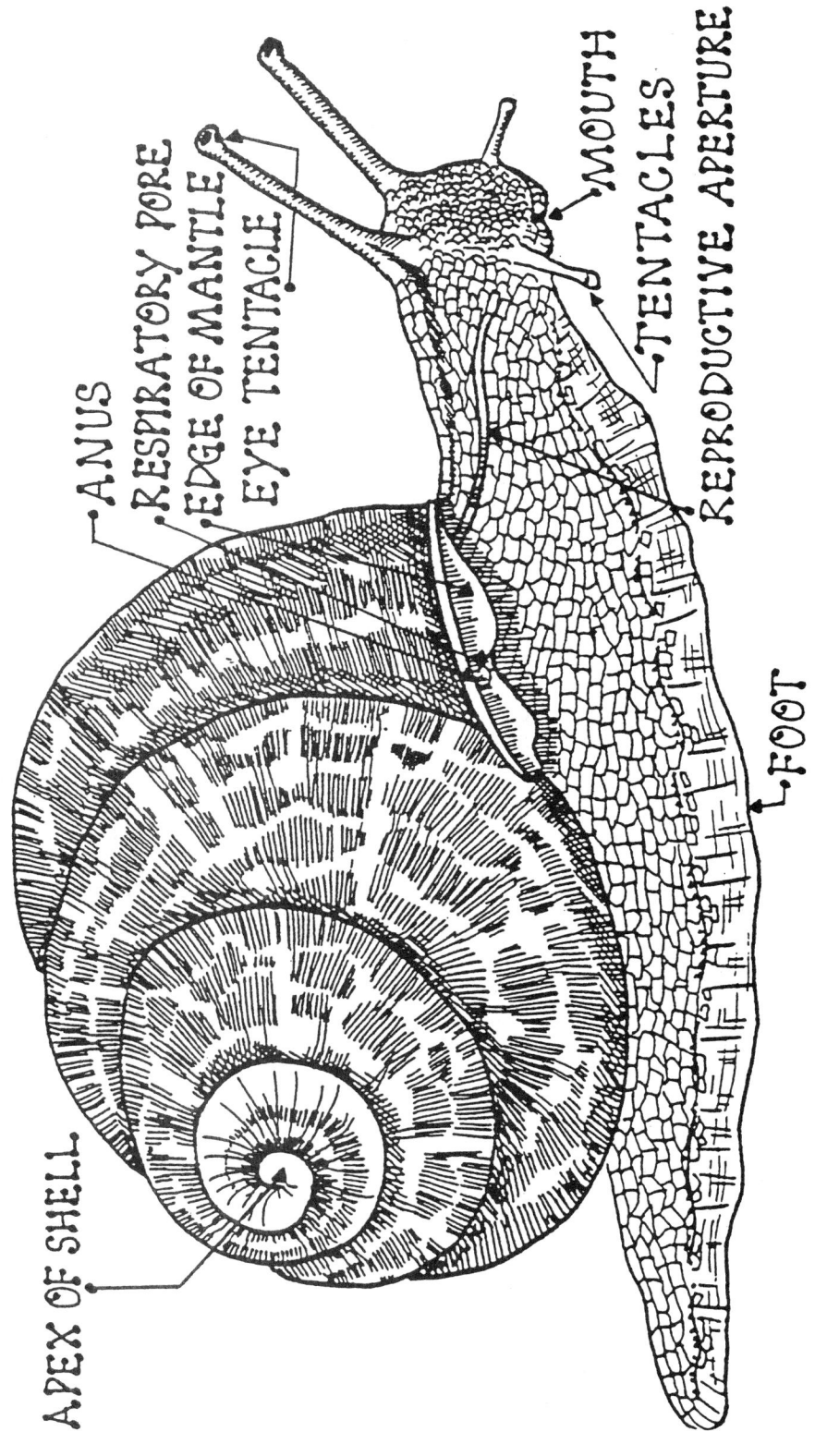

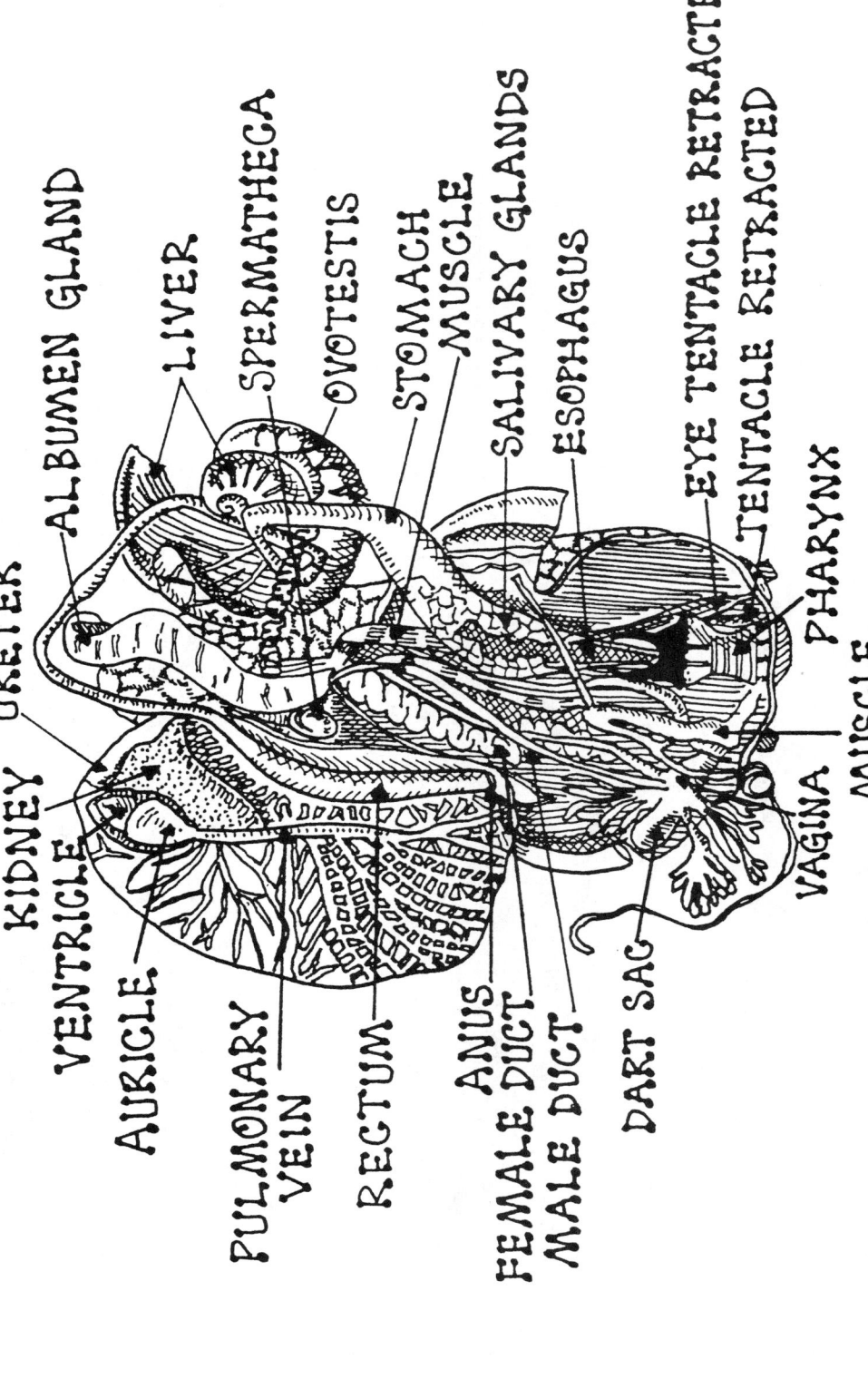

INTERNAL ANATOMY OF THE SNAIL
Helix pomatia
Class Gastropoda

INSIDE OUT

I. Topic Area
Snail anatomy

II. Introductory Statement
Students will observe the various parts of a snail and measure its height, length and mass.

III. Math Skills
a. Measuring
b. Graphing

Science Processes
a. Observing
b. Collecting & recording data

IV. Materials
one snail and one 8 or 10 oz. clear plastic cup per student
scales and masses
rulers
scotch tape
activity sheets
scissors
crayons or markers

V. Key Question
What are the main body parts of a snail?

VI. Background Information
See snail fact sheets.

VII. Management Suggestions
1. Secure at least sixty snails for this lesson and the ones that follow. They are easy to find at night in most gardens near ground cover and wet areas. They can be kept in a covered container (with air holes) and fed lettuce.
2. The ruler on the activity sheet can be cut out and taped to the inside of a clear plastic 10 oz. cup so that it can be read from the outside. Snails will climb a cup (or any object) if it is placed in front of them. As the snail moves up the cup, he stretches out and is easily measured without any handling. Note: the cup should be taped to the desk to prevent it from tipping over as the snail climbs it.
3. Get as many scales as you can to speed up the massing process. Most garden snails will have a mass of approximately 5 to 10 grams. If gram masses are not available, paperclips, or other lightweight, uniform objects can be used.

VIII. Procedure
1. Tell the class that they will be observing the external parts of common garden snails.
2. Pass out the activity sheet, a snail and a clear plastic cup and ruler to each student.
3. Have students observe their snails and see if they can find the six parts listed on the sheet. Encourage them to share any other observations they make.
4. Discuss the measurement procedures for finding the length, height and mass of the snails. Have the students make these measurements and complete the activity sheet.
5. Have students share the lengths, heights and masses of their snails. This information can be recorded on the chalkboard or on a chart and graphed.
6. **Make sure children wash their hands after handling the snails.**
7. After the external features of the snails have been observed and the snails have been returned to their home, pass out the "Body of a Snail" activity sheet.
8. Fold the paper in half along the center line so that the top half (body parts list) folds behind the bottom half which shows the snail's internal organs.
9. Cut out the outline of the snail along the dotted lines making sure not to cut the sections so marked.
10. Open the paper back up and pick a color for each of the parts listed in the key. Color in the key and the corresponding body parts with the colors chosen.
11. Fold the paper so that the printed part is now on the inside. Have students draw the outside features of the snail on the outside of the paper producing a model of a snail that can be opened up to show the internal organs.

IX. Discussion Questions
1. Did the snails all look alike or were there individual differences that could be recognized?
2. How does the snail's anatomy compare to that of other animals or humans?
3. What things were you able to observe about your snail that you have never seen before?

X. Extended Activities
1. Try to find a way to distinguish individual snails.
2. Make a bar graph of the lengths, heights and masses of all the snails.

XI. Curriculum Coordinates
Language Arts:
Brainstorm adjectives describing the snails. Write snail poems.
Research:
Look up information on the various types of snails and their geographic locations.
Math:
Measure the circumference of the snail's shells. Compare the length of the foot to the total length.

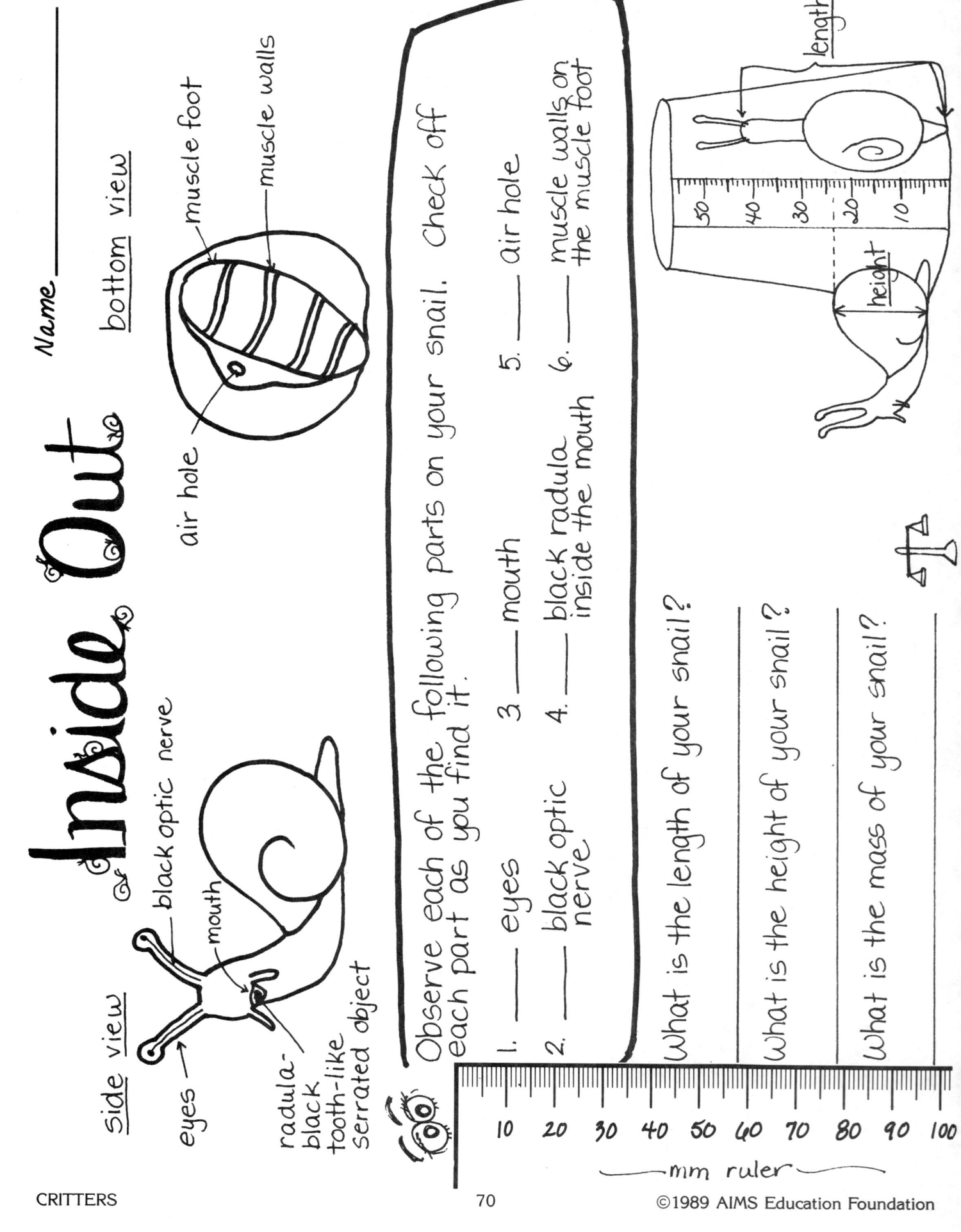

The Body of a Snail - Key

- ☐ A – Eyes
- ☐ B – Tentacles
- ☐ C – Mouth
- ☐ D – Nerve Centers
- ☐ E – Stomach
- ☐ F – Salivary Gland
- ☐ G – Kidney
- ☐ H – Heart
- ☐ I – Shell
- ☐ J – Intestine
- ☐ K – Ducts of Digestive Gland
- ☐ L – Digestive Gland
- ☐ M – Tail
- ☐ N – Foot

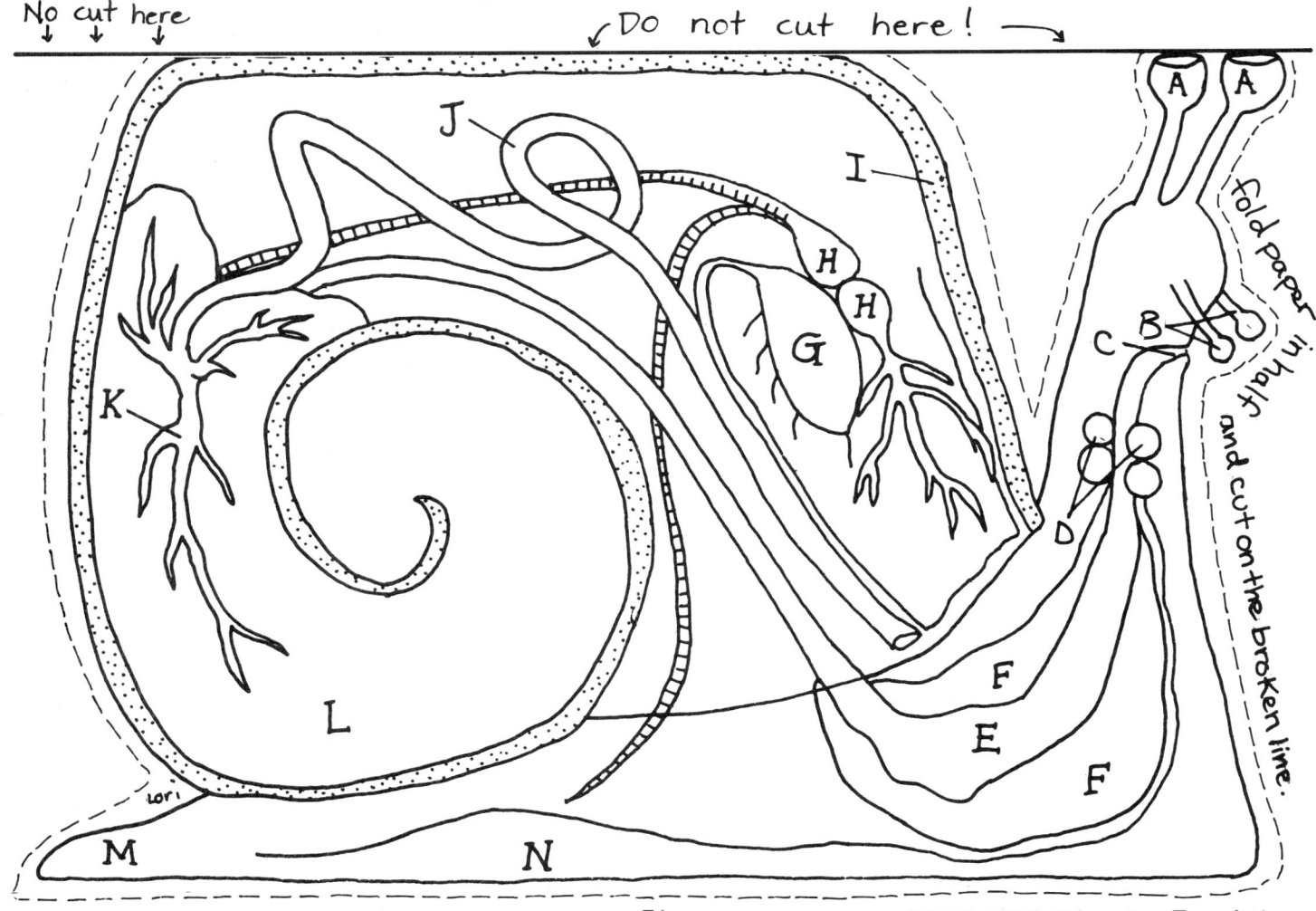

CRITTERS © 1989 AIMS Education Foundation

PORTRAIT OF AN AVERAGE SNAIL

I. Topic Area
Snails

II. Introductory Statement
Students will make quantitative and comparative observations of garden snails.

III. Math Skills
  a. Measuring
  b. Averaging
  c. Graphing

Science Processes
  a. Observing
  b. Collecting & organizing data
  c. Classifying

IV. Materials
snails
clear plastic cups
activity sheets
water bottles
balance and masses
rulers
white-out or nail polish

V. Key Question
How would you describe the average garden snail?

VI. Background Information
See fact sheets on snails.

VII. Management Suggestions
1. Allow several days for students to collect and bring in snails so that there are enough for each student to have one.
2. Mark each snail with white-out or nail polish so that it can be identified. A dot of white-out with a student number written in pen on the dot works well.
3. Have a large box with a lid in the classroom for keeping the snails.
4. Review how to calculate averages and surface area, if necessary.
5. For the stretching out measurement, allow snails to climb a vertical surface.
6. Have students work in groups of four for this activity.
7. Snails like to climb. If the plastic cup is placed upside down in their path they will climb it, making it easy to measure them stretched out.
8. If you don't have rulers, the paper ruler on the activity sheet can be cut out and taped to the inside of the cup (with the zero mark at the lip of the cup) allowing students to measure both the height and the length of the snails.
9. If gram masses are not available the snails can be weighed using paper clips or other small uniform objects.
10. The total surface area of the snail will be hard to calculate. You may wish to have the students just trace the profile of the snail (side view) on the grid and find the surface area of the profile instead.

VIII. Procedure
1. Tell the students that each group will find the average mass, surface area, length and height for their group of snails.
2. Pass out the first two activity sheets and discuss them.
3. Have each group do each of the four measurements and fill in the first two activity sheets. They will find an average length, height, mass and surface area for their snails.
4. When all the groups have finished finding their averages and recording that information, pass out the third activity sheet and complete it together as a total class activity.
5. Discuss the results.

IX. Discussion Questions
1. Discuss what students learned about the average snails measurements.
2. Discuss other quantitative information about snails that might be explored.
3. Discuss whether or not the class findings could be used to predict what garden snails are like in other locations.
4. Discuss the factors that might affect the snails measurements.
5. Discuss ways to get more accurate measurements.

X. Extended Activities
1. Take a larger sample of snails and compare results. Perhaps two classes can do the activity and share data.

XI. Curriculum Coordinates
Language:
Write a story about the life of an average snail.

Geography:
Research snails and find out where they live around the world. Make a map showing your findings.

Science:
Try to find a way to keep snails out of your garden without using pesticides.

PORTRAIT OF AN AVERAGE SNAIL

Name _____

Station A — Stretching Out (length)

snail #	prediction	length
	cm	cm
	cm	cm
	cm	cm
	cm	cm

_____ cm ÷ 4 = _____ cm
total lengths   average

Station B — Standing Tall (height)

snail #	prediction	height
	cm	cm
	cm	cm
	cm	cm
	cm	cm

centimeter tape

_____ cm ÷ 4 = _____ cm
total heights   average

CRITTERS   ©1989 AIMS Education Foundation

PORTRAIT OF AN AVERAGE SNAIL

Station C — Weighing in (mass)

snail #	prediction	mass
	g	g
	g	g
	g	g
	g	g

_____ g ÷ 4 = _____ g
total grams   average

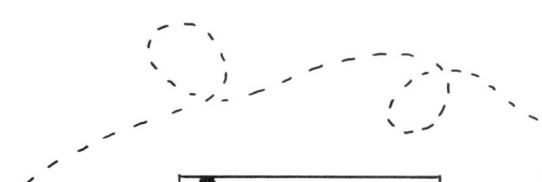

Station D — Squaring Off

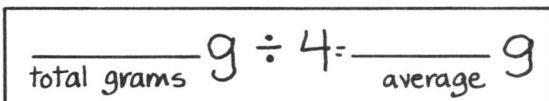

snail #	prediction	surface area
	cm²	cm²
	cm²	cm²
	cm²	cm²
	cm²	cm²

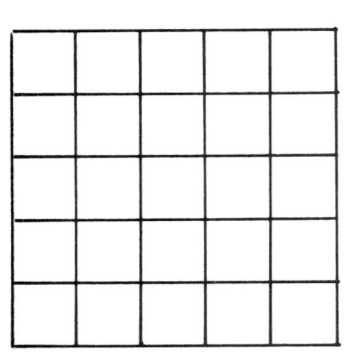

cm grid

_____ cm² ÷ 4 = _____ cm²
total surface   average
   areas

CRITTERS   ©1989 AIMS Education Foundation

Name _____

PORTRAIT OF AN AVERAGE SNAIL

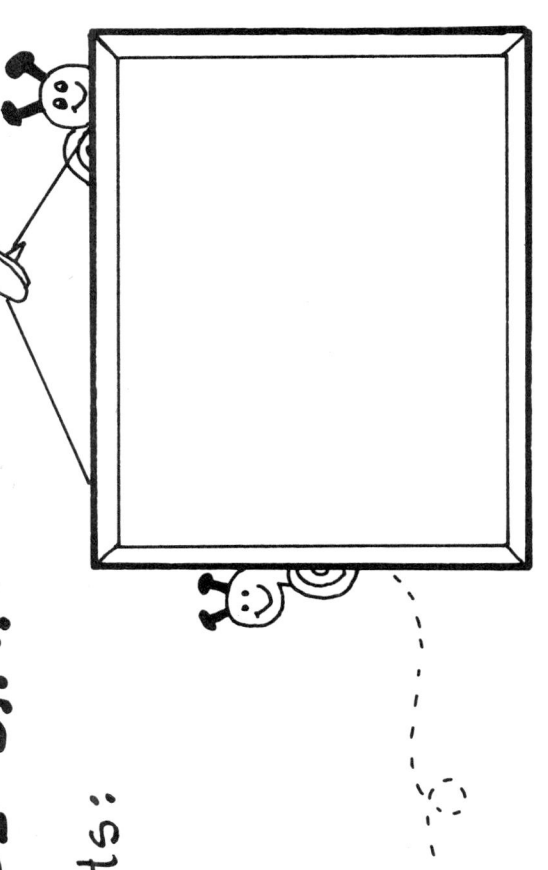

#1 My Group's Average Measurements:

_____ length
_____ height
_____ mass
_____ surface area

#2 Draw a scale drawing of your snail using the length and height measurements.

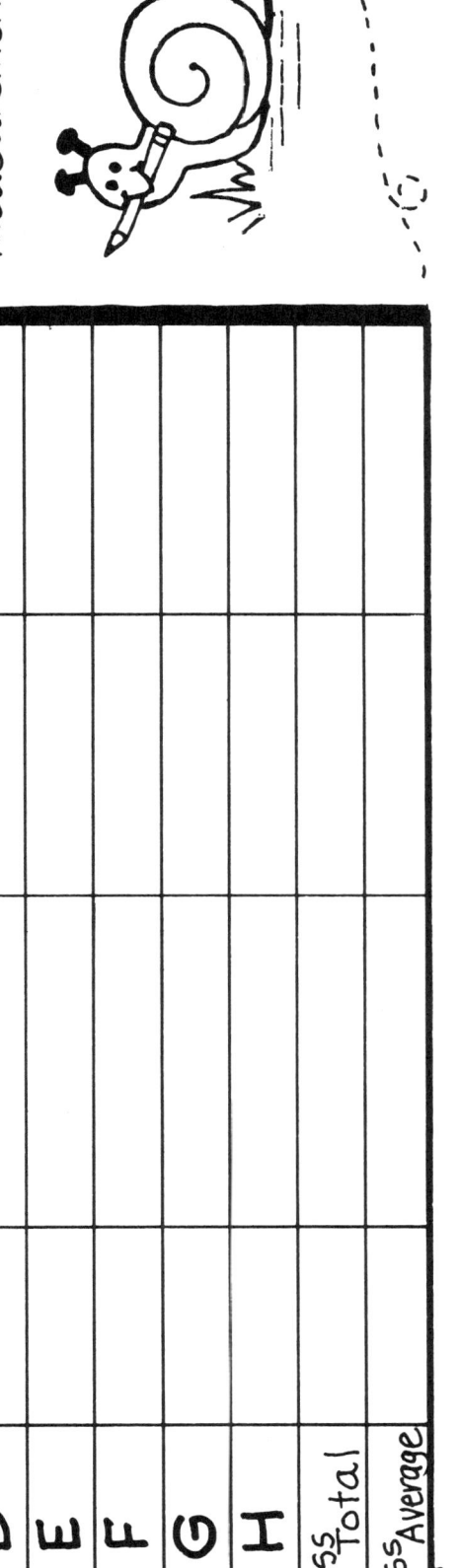

Let's Compare Averages:

Group	Mass	Surface Area	Length	Height
A				
B				
C				
D				
E				
F				
G				
H				
Class Total				
Class Average				

CRITTERS   ©1989 AIMS Education Foundation

THE SLIME TRAIL

I. Topic Area
Snail's rate of travel

II. Introductory Statement
Students will determine whether the big snails or small snails travel faster.

III. Math Skills
a. Measuring
b. Multiplying
c. Graphing
d. Problem solving

Science Processes
a. Observing
b. Collecting & organizing data
c. Predicting

IV. Materials
large and small snails
activity sheets
string
meter sticks or meter tapes (upper grades)
large sheets of dark construction or butcher paper
scissors and tape
watch with second hand

V. Key Question
Will a big or small snail travel farther in an hour?

VI. Background Information
Snails move very slowly. The common garden snail travels an average of three meters per hour. The snail has tiny glands in its flat muscular foot that secrete a layer of shiny slime. This layer of slime is put down as a road for the snail to travel on and allows the snail to travel over loose or day surfaces that would otherwise stick to its moist foot. If you watch a snail move, you can see the muscles in its foot move like waves.

VII. Management Suggestions
1. Make sure you have enough big and small snails so that each group has one of each.
2. This activity can be done in groups of 2-4 students.
3. This activity can be done at the primary level using the first activity sheet, which measures the distance snails travel in two minutes using pieces of string, or at the upper grade level using the second activity sheet which has students doing three trials and finding the average distance traveled in one minute time periods.
4. The activity sheets "A Trip to Snail World" and "The Up or Down Snail" are included in this lesson as extension activities for older students.

VIII. Procedure
1. Pass out the activity sheet and have students predict which snail will travel farther in two minutes (primary) or one minute (upper), a big or small one.
2. Pass out a big and small snail, two pieces of string and a large, dark piece of paper to each group.
3. Students will put the big snail on the paper and draw a line behind the snail. As soon as the snail starts moving begin timing a two (or one) minute interval.
4. When the time is up draw a second line behind the snail and then remove it from the paper. Lay one of the pieces of string along the path that the snail took (which will be visible because of the slime trail left on the paper) from the first line to the second line. This string can be cut to the correct length (primary activity) or marked and placed along a meter stick or tape to get the distance traveled in centimeters (upper grade activity).
5. Turn the sheet of dark paper over and repeat the process with the small snail.
6. Primary students can then make a direct comparison of the two strings and answer the question of which snail traveled farther in two minutes. The groups should share results and the two strings from each group can be taped to a bulletin board graph showing the distances traveled by the big and small snails.
7. Upper grade students should repeat the above process two more times, finding the average distance each snail travels in two minutes by collecting the data from three trials for each snail.
8. Fill in the activity sheet and discuss the results.

IX. Discussion Questions
1. Discuss why snails leave a slime trail.
2. Discuss the results of the activity and whether any conclusions can be made.

X. Extended Activities
1. Primary students may want to repeat the activity and compare results with the first trial.
2. Older students can do the "A Trip to Snail World" activity sheet using the average speed determined for their snails.
3. The snails vertical and horizontal speeds can be determined using the format presented in the activity sheet "The Up or Down Snail."

XI. Curriculum Coordinates
Art:
Make a picture from the slime trails by painting over them.

Science:
Research the snail and find out what the slime trail is and why the snail leaves it behind when he moves.

THE SLIME TRAIL

Name _____

STOP AFTER ONE MINUTE.

	DISTANCE PREDICTION	TEST 1	TEST 2	TEST 3	AVERAGE
BIG SNAIL	___ cm	___ cm/min	___ cm/min	___ cm/min	___ cm/min
LITTLE SNAIL	___ cm	___ cm/min	___ cm/min	___ cm/min	___ cm/min

BIG SNAIL'S RATE: AVERAGE CM ___ × 60 = ___ cm per hour ÷ 100 = ___ meters per hour

LITTLE SNAIL'S RATE: AVERAGE CM ___ × 60 = ___ cm per hour ÷ 100 = ___ meters per hour

1. HOW LONG WOULD IT TAKE THE BIG SNAIL TO TRAVEL **10** METERS?

   FORMULA: DISTANCE ÷ RATE = TIME   10 meters ÷ ___ meters per hour = ___ hours.

2. HOW LONG WOULD IT TAKE THE LITTLE SNAIL TO TRAVEL **20** METERS?

   FORMULA: DISTANCE ÷ RATE = TIME   20 meters ÷ ___ meters per hour = ___ hours.

CRITTERS

©1989 AIMS Education Foundation

A TRIP TO SNAIL WORLD

BIG SNAIL AVERAGE _____ MPH
METERS PER HOUR

SAMMY'S AVERAGE _____ MPH
METERS PER HOUR

1. How long will it take for each of the snails to get to SNAIL WORLD?

   BETSY BIG SNAIL _____

   SAMMY SMALL SNAIL _____

2. Who will arrive first? _____

3. At the end of the day, both snails were very tired so they took the "SHORT CUT" road home to SAMMY'S house.

   • How long did it take SAMMY to reach his home? _____

   • How long did it take BETSY to reach SAMMY'S house? _____

   • What is the difference? _____

CRITTERS ©1989 AIMS Education Foundation

THE UP OR DOWN SNAIL

I. Topic Area
Snails

II. Introductory Statement
Students will determine the rates that snails travel on horizontal and vertical surfaces.

III. Math Skills
a. Measuring
b. Computation
c. Averaging
d. Graphing
e. Rates

Science Processes
a. Observing
b. Collecting & organizing data
c. Predicting
d. Controlling variables
e. Generalizing

IV. Materials
snails
activity sheets
pieces of cardboard (8" x 12" or bigger)
watch or clock with second hand
string and centimeter rulers or tapes

V. Key Question
Does a snail go faster on a flat surface or a vertical one?

VI. Background Information
See snail fact sheets.

VII. Management Suggestions
1. Make sure you have enough snails for each group or student to have one. You might need a few extra snails in case some of them are sluggish.
2. To get snails moving you can put them in a box or bag and place the bag on an overhead projector. Turn on the projector for a few minutes and the warmth from the lamp will get the cold-blooded snails moving, but will not harm them.
3. Dampening the table and ramp will also encourage the snails to move.
4. This activity works well with students in groups of 2-4.
5. Each group will need a cardboard ramp for their snail.

VIII. Procedure
1. Introduce the activity by asking students whether it is easier for them to walk on level ground or to climb up stairs or a hill? Ask them to predict whether a snail would go faster on a level surface or a vertical one.
2. Review the formula for finding rate:
    Rate = Distance / Time.
3. Pass out the activity sheet and discuss it with the students.
4. Divide the students into groups and give each group a snail and a ramp.
5. Have the groups use the classroom clock or a watch with a second hand to time the snail for one minute on a flat surface. The timing should begin as soon as the snail starts moving.
6. At the end of one minute, the distance the snail moved should be measured in centimeters and recorded on the activity sheet.
7. This process should be repeated two more times and the average rate the snail travels on horizontal surfaces can be calculated in centimeters/minute.
8. Set up the cardboard so that it is vertical and place the snail at its base. As soon as the snail begins climbing, time it for one minute. At the end of one minute find the distance traveled and record it on the activity sheet. Repeat this procedure two more times to find the average rate that the snail travels on a vertical surface.
9. Fill in the rest of the activity sheet and share group results with the class.

IX. Discussion Questions
1. Discuss why it is harder for people to climb hills than it is to walk on level surfaces.
2. Discuss why some animals, like snails, are able to climb vertical surfaces.
3. Discuss the findings of the groups. Draw conclusions.
4. Discuss other variables, such as the surface that the snail climbs, that might affect the results.

SNAIL OBSERVER: _____

THE UP OR DOWN SNAIL

QUESTION: CAN A SNAIL TRAVEL AT A FASTER RATE ON A FLAT OR VERTICAL SURFACE?

PREDICT _____

$$RATE = \frac{DISTANCE\ THE\ SNAIL\ TRAVELS}{TIME}$$

$$R = \frac{D}{T}$$

VERTICAL SURFACE

*USE a string to measure the slime trail to determine the distance the snail travels in one minute.

TRIAL	DISTANCE	÷	TIME	=	RATE
#1		÷	1 min.	=	____ cm/min.
#2		÷	1 min.	=	____ cm/min.
#3		÷	1 min.	=	____ cm/min.
				TOTAL RATE	____

TOTAL RATE ÷ 3 = AVERAGE RATE
____ ÷ 3 = ____ cm/min.

FLAT SURFACE

TRIAL:	DISTANCE	÷	TIME	=	RATE
#1		÷	1 min.	=	____ cm/min
#2		÷	1 min.	=	____ cm/min
#3		÷	1 min.	=	____ cm/min
				TOTAL RATE	____

TOTAL RATE ÷ 3 = AVERAGE RATE
____ ÷ 3 = ____ cm/min.

*The flat surface average rate was _____ the average vertical rate.
>, <, =

CRITTERS   81   ©1989 AIMS Education Foundation

WHAT'S YOUR ANGLE?

I. Topic Area
Snails

II. Introductory Statement
Students will determine how the angle of a ramp affects the rate at which a snail pulls a load up the ramp.

III. Math Skills
a. Measuring
b. Computation
c. Averaging
d. Graphing
e. Rates

Science Processes
a. Observing
b. Collecting & organizing data
c. Predicting
d. Controlling variables
e. Generalizing

IV. Materials
snails
activity sheets
pieces of cardboard (8" x 12" or bigger)
watch or clock with second hand
string and centimeter rulers or tapes
thread, tape and paper clips
scale (optional)

V. Key Question
How does the angle affect the rate at which a snail pulls a load up a ramp?

VI. Background Information
See snail fact sheets.

VII. Management Suggestions
1. Make sure you have enough snails for each group or student to have one. You might need a few extra snails in case some of them are sluggish.
2. To get snails moving you can put them in a box or bag and place the bag on an overhead projector. Turn on the projector for a few minutes and the warmth from the lamp will get the cold-blooded snails moving, but will not harm them.
3. Dampening the ramp will also encourage the snails to move.
4. This activity works well with students in groups of 2-4.
5. Each group will need a cardboard ramp for their snail.

VIII. Procedure
1. Introduce the activity by asking students if they could pull their own weight along a flat surface, up a ramp or straight up the side of a building. Tell them that the activity they will be doing will show if snails can pull their weight on a flat surface, up a ramp and straight up a vertical surface. They will be finding the difference in the rate at which the snail is able to do these things.
2. Pass out the activity sheet and discuss it. Demonstrate how to construct ramps of 30, 60 and 90 degrees using the angle finder on the activity sheet.
3. Review the timing and measuring procedures and how to calculate the rate the snail travels in centimeters per minute.
4. Divide the class into groups and give each group a snail, a cardboard ramp, a piece of string and a ruler (or a tape measure), some thread, paper clips, and tape.
5. Have the groups weigh their snails using paper clips (if scales are not available, they can estimate the weight—about 6 to 10 paper clips).
6. Tie the paper clips to the thread and tape the other end to the snail's shell so that the paper clips are a few centimeters behind the snail.
7. Place the snail and its load on the flat piece of cardboard. Make a mark behind the snail. As soon as it starts moving, time it for one minute. At the end of one minute, make another mark behind the snail and measure the distance the snail moved. Use this information to find the rate the snail traveled on a flat surface and fill it in on the activity sheet.
8. Set up the cardboard to make a ramp with a 30 degree angle. Place the snail on the ramp and repeat the above procedures to find the rate and record it on the activity sheet.
9. Repeat the above process for ramps of 60 and 90 degrees. Using the information from your chart complete the line graph on the activity sheet. Share group results with the class and discuss.

IX. Discussion Questions
1. Discuss the similarities and differences in the group results. Why do you think this happened?
2. Talk about ways to control variables and get more consistent results.
3. Discuss the effect of the size of the snails on the results.
4. Talk about other creatures that are able to carry their own weight.
5. Discuss the relationship of these results to the invention of the inclined plane.

X. Extended Activities
1. Find the maximum number of paper clips a snail can pull on level surfaces, or up various ramps.
2. Find out how many times its own weight a snail can pull.
3. Test the effect of the load a snail pulls on its rate.
4. Try other ramp angles.

XI. Curriculum Coordinates
Art:
Put some snails in a pan with some colored water (colored with food coloring) that just covers the bottom of the pan. The food coloring will not hurt them. Then place the snails on a piece of white paper and they will leave colored trails. Put several snails with different colors on the paper for fantastic results.

Language Arts:
Students can compose snail poems and write them on the colored snail trails.

Geography:
Research the different places snails are found around the world. There are over 80,000 varieties found on earth.

What's Your Angle?

Question: HOW DOES THE ANGLE OF THE RAMP AFFECT THE RATE AT WHICH A SNAIL PULLS A LOAD UP THE RAMP?

Predict: AT WHICH ANGLE DO YOU THINK THE SNAIL WILL TRAVEL THE FASTEST? _____
WHY? _____

ANGLE:	DISTANCE	÷	TIME	=	RATE
FLAT (0°)	_____ cm.	÷	1 min.	=	_____ cm/min
30°	_____ cm.	÷	1 min	=	_____ cm/min
60°	_____ cm.	÷	1 min	=	_____ cm/min.
90°	_____ cm.	÷	1 min	=	_____ cm/min.

CRITTERS

©1989 AIMS Education Foundation

SNAIL OLYMPICS

I. Topic Area
Snails

II. Introductory Statement
Students will have their snail compete in four Olympic style events.

III. Math Skills
a. Measuring
b. Counting
c. Computation

Science Processes
a. Observing
b. Collecting & organizing data

IV. Materials
snails
activity sheets
string
pencils
large plastic cups
tape
cardboard tube sections (about 1" long)
water bottle

V. Key Question
What does a snail do when it encounters obstacles in its path?

VI. Background Information
Snails will often climb over objects put in their path instead of going around them. They will also tend to climb up vertical and near vertical surfaces. Snails need a moist environment to survive and will tend to follow a damp trail on an otherwise dry surface. Since snails are cold-blooded, they will be more active when they are warm.

VII. Management Suggestions
1. Make sure you have enough snails so that each group or student has one.
2. This activity can be done individually or in groups of 2-4 students.
3. The events can be done individually or together in an Olympic format.
4. The snails can be made more active by squirting water on them and placing them in a warm (not hot) location.
5. To get the snails to follow a path, the dry surface can be moistened with a water bottle.

VIII. Procedure
1. Set up the events as shown on the activity sheet. The top of a table, or a tile floor are good places for the Olympics.
2. For the big race snails are placed on the starting line. They are allowed to travel in any direction. At the end of three minutes their position is marked and their slime trails can be measured using a piece of string or a tape measure. A sheet of dark paper placed on the table will highlight the slime trail and make measuring it easier.
3. To set up the hurdles, place pencils 5 centimeters apart on a flat surface. To get the snails to go in a somewhat straight line over the hurdles, a water bottle can be used to create a damp path which the snails will hopefully follow.
4. For the mountain climbing event place the snail near an inverted cup that is taped to the table or floor.
5. For the tunneling event, space the tubes about 5 centimeters apart. The tubes may have to be moved to get the snails to go through them. They may also want to climb the tube instead of go through it. This event is the most difficult one to get the snails to cooperate.
6. After the events are completed the points can be tabulated and the winning snail can be determined.
7. Complete the activity sheet and discuss the results.

IX. Discussion Questions
1. Discuss what the tendency of snails is when they meet obstacles. Do they prefer to go over, through, or around objects in their paths?
2. What event was your snail best at? Worst? Why do you think this happened?

X. Extended Activities
1. Try the Olympics again and see what you can do to help your snail get better scores.
2. Older students can do the "A Snail's Pace" activities using the activity sheet provided.

Name _____

Snail Olympics

Events:	How to:		Total:
1. Big Race:	Start ᘛ⁐̤ᕐᐷ ----? 3 min. race Distance	1 pt per cm	___
2. Hurdles:	Count the # of pencils the snail goes over in 3 min. 5pts 5pts	5 pts per pencil	___
3. Mountain Climbing:	Less than 2 minutes = More than 2 minutes =	20 pts 10 pts	___
4. Tunneling:	5pts 5pts 3 min race	5 pts per tube	___
		Total Points:	___

1. What was your snail's best event? _____

2. Observations: What happened when the snail saw the pencil? _____

3. What happened when the snail saw the toilet paper tubes? _____

CRITTERS   85   ©1989 AIMS Education Foundation

A Snail's Pace

Take a well rested snail who seems ready to travel and calculate the rate of speed at which it is moving. Use an unobstructed flat area. Take three samples on a horizontal surface and three on a vertical surface to determine if there is any noticable difference.

$$\text{RATE} = \text{distance} \div \text{time}$$

HORIZONTAL SURFACE

Trial	TIME	DISTANCE	RATE
1	sec.	cm	cm/sec
2	sec.	cm	cm/sec
3	sec.	cm	cm/sec
average rate =			cm/sec

VERTICAL SURFACE

Trial	TIME	DISTANCE	RATE
1	sec.	cm	cm/sec
2	sec.	cm	cm/sec
3	sec.	cm	cm/sec
average rate =			cm/sec

Compare your results and describe any noticable difference in the rate of travel on the different planes.

A Snail's Pace   Name_____

A snail track team is participating in a track meet in which a gold medal is awarded for first place, a silver medal for second, and a bronze medal for third.

You may enter two snails from your team in all except the relays. Enter a team of four snails in the relay and find their average rate. The rate is found by dividing the distance by the time in seconds.

Event	Team Member	Total Time	Rate mm/sec.	Rate cm/sec.
100 mm dash				
100 mm low hurdles				
100 mm vertical climb				
100 mm ramp climb				
100 mm barrel roll				
400 mm relay				
Team Total				
Team Average				

CRITTERS

SILKWORMS

Beautiful silk fabrics come from small, off-white, colored silkmoths. These insects are raised commercially on silkworm farms. Like many insects they have a 4 stage life cycle beginning as an egg. It is easy to watch the complete life cycle in the classroom as long as there is a Mulberry tree nearby.

Once new spring leaves appear on a Mulberry tree, the small eggs may be set on fresh leaves in an uncovered box. Within 3 weeks the eggs will begin to hatch into black silkworms about the size of a comma. Be sure the small silkworms have fresh Mulberry leaves every day, removing dried out leaves. They will grow quickly. Once the silkworms are large enough to see easily you can place a screen or netting with fresh leaves on top of the old ones.

The silkworms will crawl through to the new leaves and make it easy to dispose of the used ones. Silkworms will continue eating for 25-30 days, ultimately becoming 10,000 times bigger than when hatched. When the silkworm is ready to spin a cocoon it will stop eating and move its head back and forth repeatedly. You may want to provide small branches on which the cocoon can be spun.

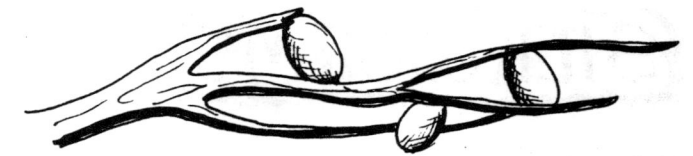

The silkworm will use the spinneret under its mouth to make a support strand of silk. Next, its body will become a U-shape and the silkworm will make figure 8 loops with its head. For 3-4 days this process continues until the cocoon is completed. Safe inside the cocoon, the silkworm molts, becoming a pupa for 10-14 days. While in the cocoon the final metamorphosis from pupa to moth gradually takes place.

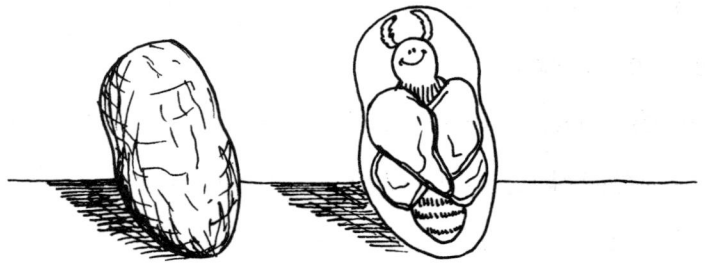

Once the metamorphosis is complete, the moth makes a small hole in the cocoon and frees itself. The adult moths cannot fly and do not eat. Their only job is to reproduce themselves by mating and laying more eggs. They may live for up to a week. Females lay between 300-500 eggs in neat rows during this time. The eggs are yellow at first but quickly change to a gray color. These eggs can be saved for the following spring by refrigerating them in baggies or small containers. There will be plenty to share with a friend!

GROWING PAINS

I. Topic Area
Silkworms

II. Introductory Statement
Students will determine if the amount of food a silkworm gets affects its growth rate.

III. Math Skills
  a. Measuring
  b. Graphing
  c. Counting
  d. Averaging

Science Processes
  a. Observing
  b. Collecting & recording data
  c. Comparing
  d. Predicting
  e. Concluding

IV. Materials
1 silkworm and container per student
fresh mulberry leaves
magnifying glass
activity sheets
ruler that measures millimeters

V. Key Question
How will the number of leaves a silkworm eats affect how much it grows?

VI. Background Information
See silkworm fact sheets.

VII. Management Suggestions
  1. Be sure there is a mulberry tree nearby or that you have access to a daily supply of fresh mulberry leaves!
  2. This activity is more easily done if you begin about 10 days after silkworms emerge. They are very difficult to measure prior to this time.
  3. Remind students to always handle the silkworms gently.
  4. Plan to collect data for about two weeks.
  5. Silkworm eggs may be ordered from Insect Lore Products, Inc., Box 1535, Shafter, CA 93263. The order phone number is (800) LIVE BUG. Eggs are available March through May only.

VIII. Procedure
DAY ONE
  1. Distribute one silkworm in a small container and a hand lens to each student.
  2. Allow time for observations and record on a class chart.
  3. Have students complete the observation activity sheet and discuss.
DAY TWO THROUGH SIXTEEN
  4. Discuss the key question.
  5. Determine a way to find how the amount of food affects the growth of a silkworm.
  6. Assign a special diet of either 1, 2, 3, 4, or 5 leaves per day to each student's silkworm. (Try to have equal numbers of silkworms for each diet.)
  7. Pass out the first activity sheet and explain that each student will be responsible for feeding their silkworm the proper number of leaves and measuring its length each school day.
  8. Once the first activity sheet is completed after 10 to 14 school days, all students whose silkworms had the same number of leaves each day share their data to find the average final length for that particular diet. This information should be filled in on the first activity sheet.
  9. Pass out the second activity sheet for the class results and have each group share their data and fill-in the table and line graph.

IX. Discussion Questions
  1. Did the silkworms that were fed the most grow the longest?
  2. What did your line graph tell you about the affect of the amount of food eaten on the growth of silkworms?
  3. Using your data, is it possible to predict the continued growth of a silkworm with a certain diet?

X. Extensions
  1. Try to find a pattern of growth relative to the number of leaves given.
  2. Find out if there are other Lepidopteras (moths or butterflies) that cannot fly.
  3. Compare silkworms with mealworms and butterfly larvae.
  4. Study the life cycle of the silkworm by continuing the observations begun in this activity. The life cycle can be drawn on the "Metamorphosis Wheel" found in the "My Mealworm" activity. A life cycle chart can also be made by students using a grain of rice to represent the egg, a short length of white pipe cleaner to represent the silkworm larva, a lump of cotton or an actual cocoon to represent the pupal stage and a cut out picture of a moth (from the "Missing Moths" activity) or drawing of the silkworm moth to represent the adult stage.
  5. Make a silkworm book to chronicle the life of your silkworm.

XI. Curriculum Coordinates
Art:
  Collect pieces of silk fabrics and make a display.
Research:
  Look up rayon. Tell how it is made.
Science:
  Make a list of other insects that have the same four stage life cycle.
Math:
  Count the number of moths that laid eggs and multiply by 500 to figure out approximately how many eggs were produced for the next year.

Study your silkworm carefully. Color the picture that looks the most like a real silkworm.

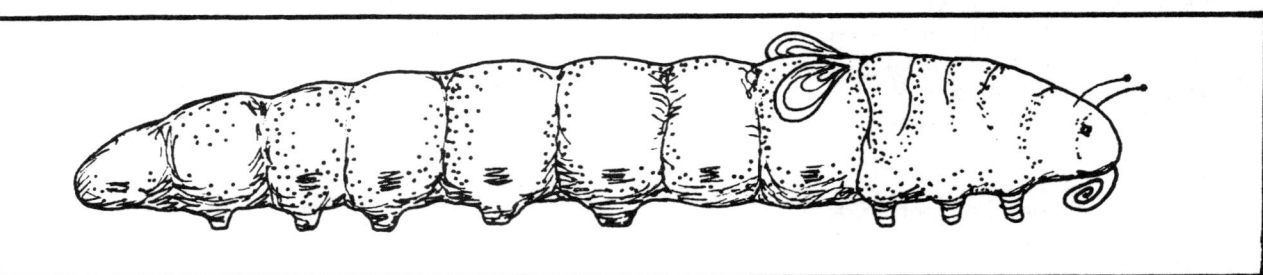

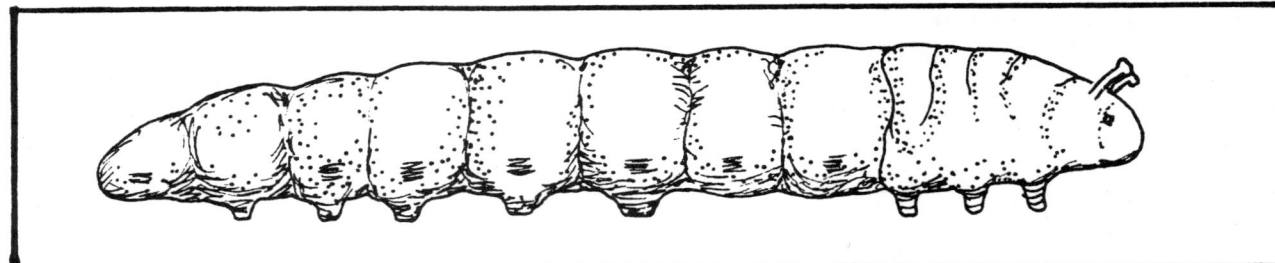

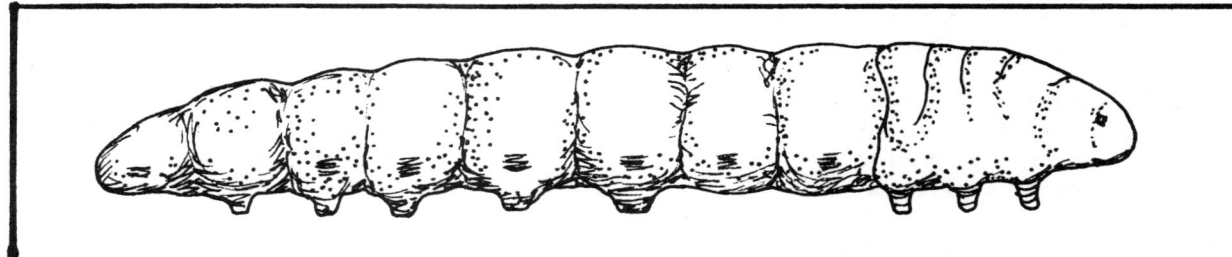

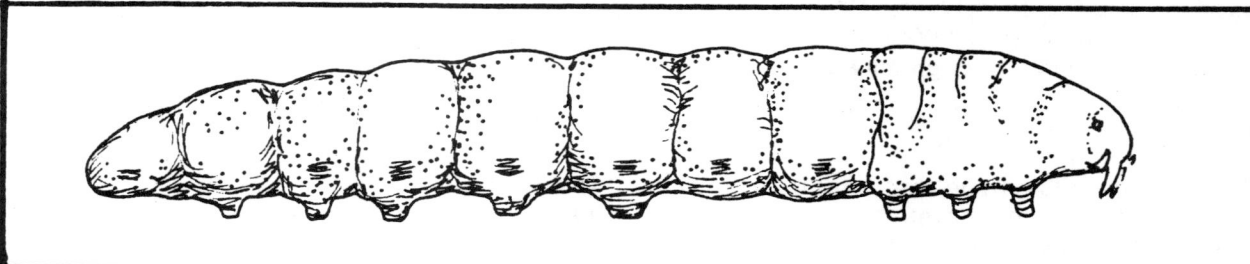

Watch your silkworm eat. What do you observe?

_____

_____

CRITTERS ©1989 AIMS Education Foundation

GROWING PAINS

Name _____

Question: Does the amount of food available affect the growth of a silkworm?

I Think _____

Color in the # of leaves you will feed

Day	Length in mm
1	mm
2	mm
3	mm
4	mm
5	mm
6	mm
7	mm
8	mm
9	mm
10	mm
11	mm
12	mm
13	mm
14	mm

Average

Dietician	Final Length
1	mm
2	mm
3	mm
4	mm
5	mm
6	mm
7	mm

+ _____

Total mm ÷ # of dieticians = Average growth

mm ruler

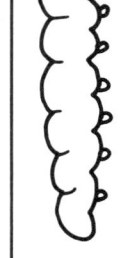

CRITTERS 93 ©1989 AIMS Education Foundation

ISOPODS

Cut a 2"x 11" strip to cover the answers. Pull down as answers are needed.

— What family do isopods belong to?

Crustaceans. Isopods are invertebrates.

— How do isopods breathe?

Through their gills.

— How many pairs of legs does a newborn isopod have?

6 pairs

— How many pairs of legs does an adult isopod have?

7 pairs

— What do isopods eat?

Anything soft, moist. They are scavengers

— Name 2 other crustaceans.

crab, shrimp, lobster

— Can isopods jump or climb?

No, they can only walk.

— When does an isopod shed its skin?

As it grows.

— Where does the female carry her eggs?

In a pouch on her underside.

— What do baby isopods look like?

They are smaller and lighter colored than adults.

CRITTERS

HOT FOOT, COLD FEET

I. **Topic Area**
   Critters response to temperature

II. **Introductory Statement**
   The students will set up an experiment in which they observe the temperature preference of isopods. This activity can also be used with other invertebrates.

III. **Math Skills**
   a. Counting
   b. Graphing
   c. Predicting

   Science Processes
   a. Observing
   b. Measuring
   c. Predicting
   d. Recording data
   e. Controlling variables

IV. **Materials**
   Per group of 4:
   3 sandwich size ziplock baggies
   1 sheet 12" x 24" aluminum foil
   10 critters: sow bugs (isopods), earthworms (night crawlers), mealworms or snails
   3 thermometers (optional)
   hot water, cold water, room temperature water
   plastic wrap

V. **Key Question**
   What temperature will the critters prefer: hot, room temperature or cold?

VI. **Background Information**
   Temperature is a very important aspect of an invertebrates environment. Invertebrate's do not have the ability to control their body temperature. As a result, their existence is dependent on the temperature of their surroundings. If the environment becomes too cool or too warm the animal cannot adjust to it and will die. Most invertebrates prefer a temperature range between 60° to 90° F. Isopods generally prefer a dark, moist and cool area (65°).

VII. **Management Suggestions**
   1. Collect enough isopods beforehand so that each group has ten. Students love to help collect isopods and can usually find them in their yards.
   2. This lesson has 2 different group tally sheets. Select the one that best addresses the ability level of your class.
   3. You may have to cover the ramp with a box to get the isopods to settle in one spot. In a bright room they tend to be too active and don't settle down.

VIII. **Procedure**
   1. Have students discuss what they already know about the critter being used. Record their responses on the board.
   2. Have them tell how they have learned about their critter. Many may respond by saying they observed much of what they know about the animals. Stress the importance of observation.
   3. Ask the key question.
   4. Explain the set up for the experiment. Set up 3 lunch baggies—one filled with ice water, one with room temperature water and the 3rd with hot tap water for each group. Remove as much air as possible from each baggie.
   * Optional: Find the temperature of each of the baggies and record it on the activity sheet next to the baggies marked: hot, room temperature and cold.
   5. Teacher:
      a. Demonstrates how to make or use the aluminum foil ramp.
      b. Demonstrate how to put critters into the center of the ramp and then cover ramp with plastic wrap. (there is enough air in the ramp for the critters when covered).
      c. Explain how to time and count the number of critters in each temperature zone and record it on the activity sheets — use the baggies as a reference point for each temperature zone.
   6. Be sure to have the students predict the number of critters that will be in each area at the end of 10 minutes.
   7. Pass out equipment, answer any questions and begin collecting and recording data.
   8. Ask each group to share their final count per temperature zone on their group sheets and graph the data.
   * Optional page 2: Compute the averages for each of the temperatures by dividing each total by the number of groups.
   9. Graph the results.
   * Optional: Upper grade students may compute the percentage found in each temperature zone and graph the results.

IX. **Discussion Question**
   Were the results consistent throughout the room? If not, what are some possible variables that could have caused these differences?

X. **Extended Activities**
   1. Students may try other "Critters" such as: night crawlers (earthworms), snails, mealworms.
   2. Students may place equal number of critters in each temperature area and see how many are in that area after 5 minutes.

XI. **Curriculum Coordinates**
   Math:
   1. Upper grades — compute the % of critters in each temperature group.
   2. In which 2 minute period was there the least amount of change in the number of critters in the *cold* temperature? Hot temperature? Room temperature?
   Language:
   Write a short commentary on what a small critter might say while choosing the best temperature to live in.
   Science:
   Research one of the following: mealworms, sow bugs (isopods), night crawlers (earthworms).

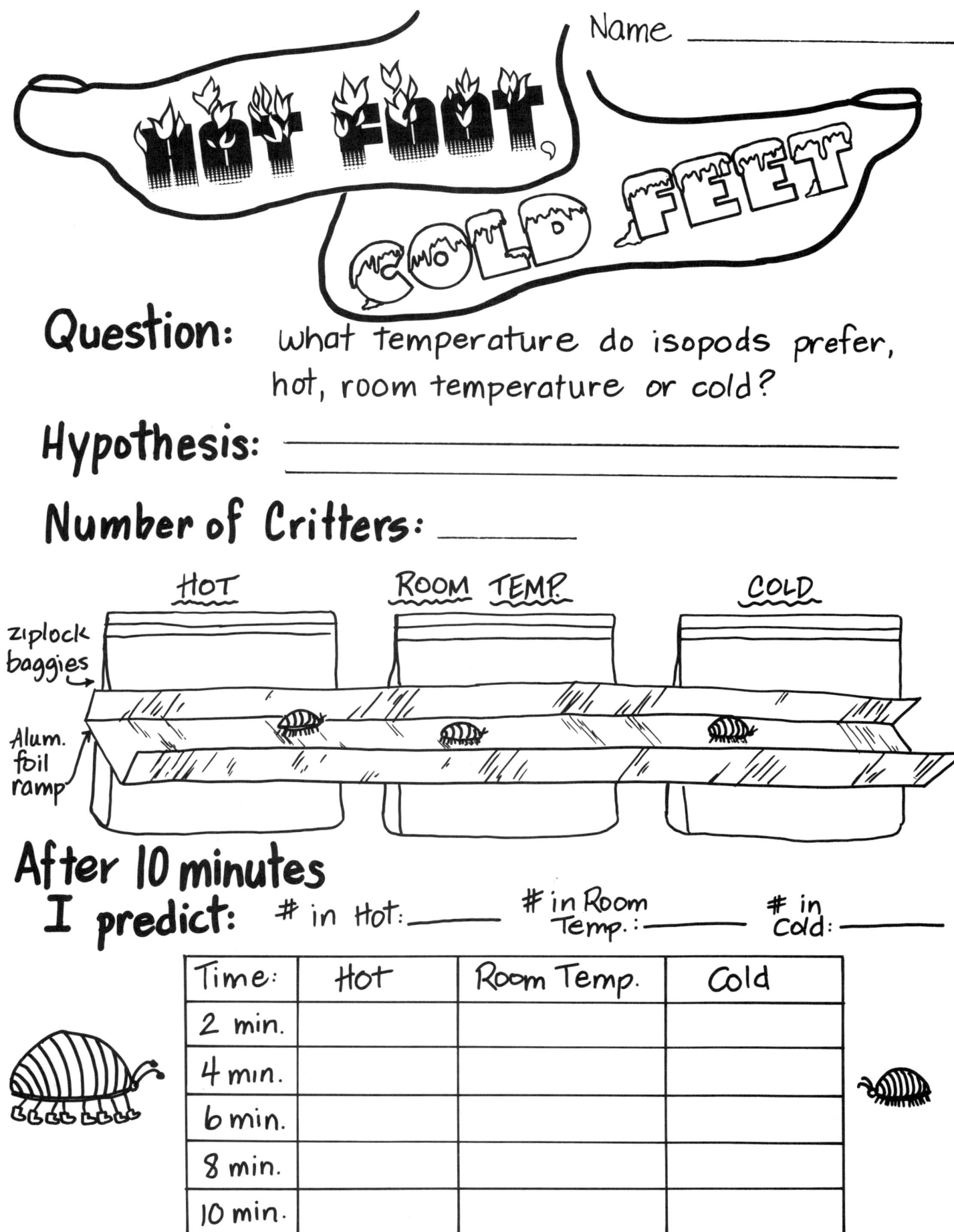

Hot Foot, Cold Feet

Results:

85		
80		
75		
70		
65		
60		
55		
50		
45		
40		
35		
30		
25		
20		
15		
10		
5		
0	Hot	Room Temp.	Cold

Number of Critters in Each Temp.

Group Tally Sheet
of Critters After 10 Minutes

Group #	Hot	Room Temp.	Cold
#1			
#2			
#3			
#4			
#5			
#6			
#7			
#8			
Class Totals			

Conclusion:

CRITTERS ©1989 AIMS Education Foundation

HOT FOOT, COLD FEET

Group Tally Sheet

① # of Critters After 10 Minutes

Group #	Hot	Room Temp.	Cold
# 1			
# 2			
# 3			
# 4			
# 5			
# 6			
# 7			
# 8			
Totals:			
÷ # of groups			
Average			

③ % of Critters in Each Temp.

Hot	Room Temp.	Cold

②

Number of critters in each Temp.	÷	Average Total # of Critters	=	Decimal Value	×	100	=	%
Hot ___	÷	___	=	.___	×	100	=	___%
Room Temp. ___	÷	___	=	.___	×	100	=	___%
Cold ___	÷	___	=	.___	×	100	=	___%

CRITTERS ©1989 AIMS Education Foundation

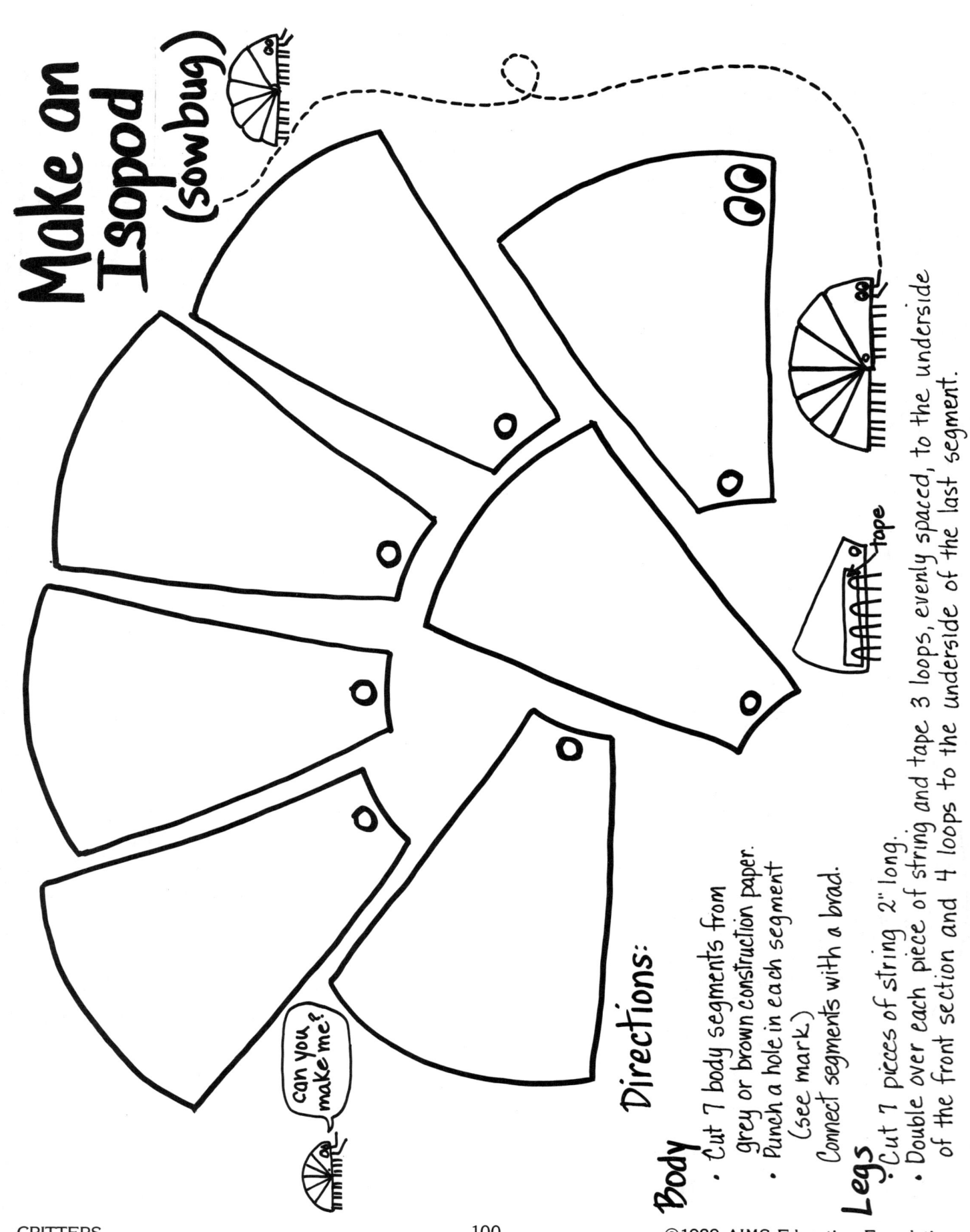

FISHFUL THINKING

I. Topic Area
Observation of goldfish

II. Introductory Statement
Students will draw a goldfish before and after observing one.

III. Math Skills
a. Computation

Science Processes
a. Observation

IV. Materials
drawing paper or activity sheet for each student
crayons
goldfish in an aquarium or in cups or jars

V. Key Question
What does a goldfish look like?

VII. Management Suggestions
Keep the goldfish out of sight until students have drawn the first picture. After the picture is drawn give the students ample opportunity to observe the goldfish before having them draw the second picture. It is best if each group has a goldfish in a jar or cup at their table.

VIII. Procedures
1. Give the students the activity sheet or a sheet of drawing paper. Ask them to fold it in half width wise and draw a line across the fold.
2. Students draw a goldfish in the top half of the paper. (Give no directions or clues of what to include).
3. Bring out goldfish in an aquarium or jars for the class to observe. Allow students to watch the goldfish throughout the day. Be sure to observe them at feeding time. After ample observation discuss what goldfish really look like and point out the various parts, such as gills, scales, fins, etc.
4. Have students draw another goldfish picture on the bottom half of drawing paper or activity sheet.
5. Compare the two drawings.
6. Students count how many new parts they included in the second picture. Record that number in the box in the lower left-hand corner.
7. Students can list the ways the two drawings are alike and the ways they are different in the blanks provided.

IX. Discussion Questions
1. How did your second picture compare to the first one?
2. Do you think it improved? Why?

X. Extended Activities
Draw other animals and redraw them after observing the actual animal or a photograph.

XI. Curriculum Coordinates
Art:
Make fish out of clay.
Language:
Write a poem about the body of a fish.

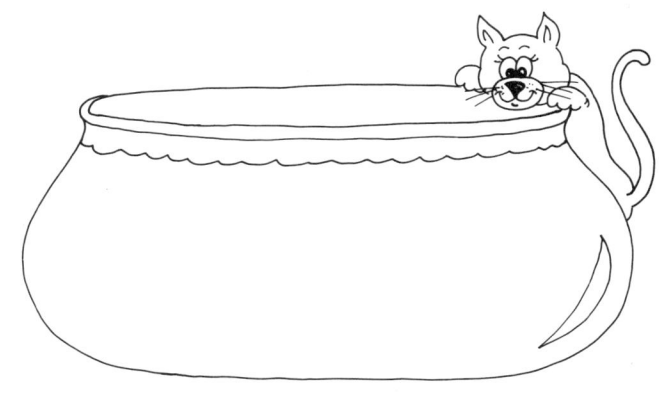

CRITTERS

©1989 AIMS Education Foundation

Fishful Thinking

Name _____

I think a goldfish looks like this.

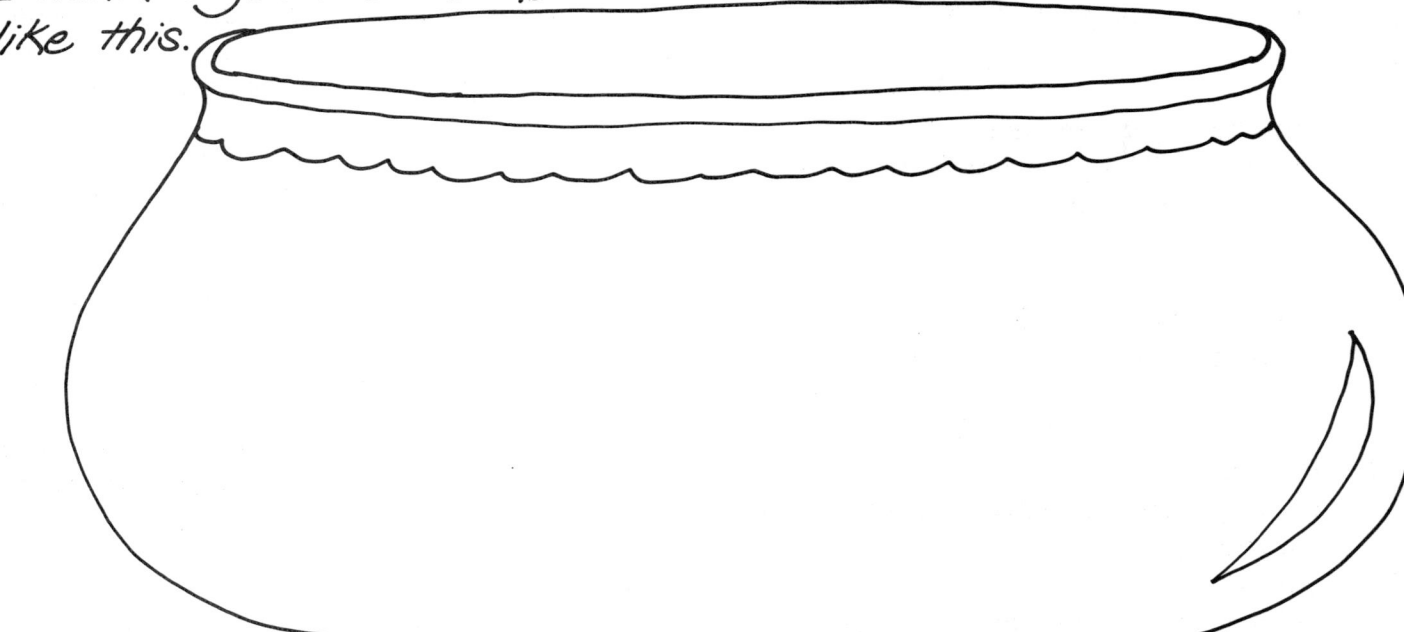

I observed a goldfish and it looks like this.

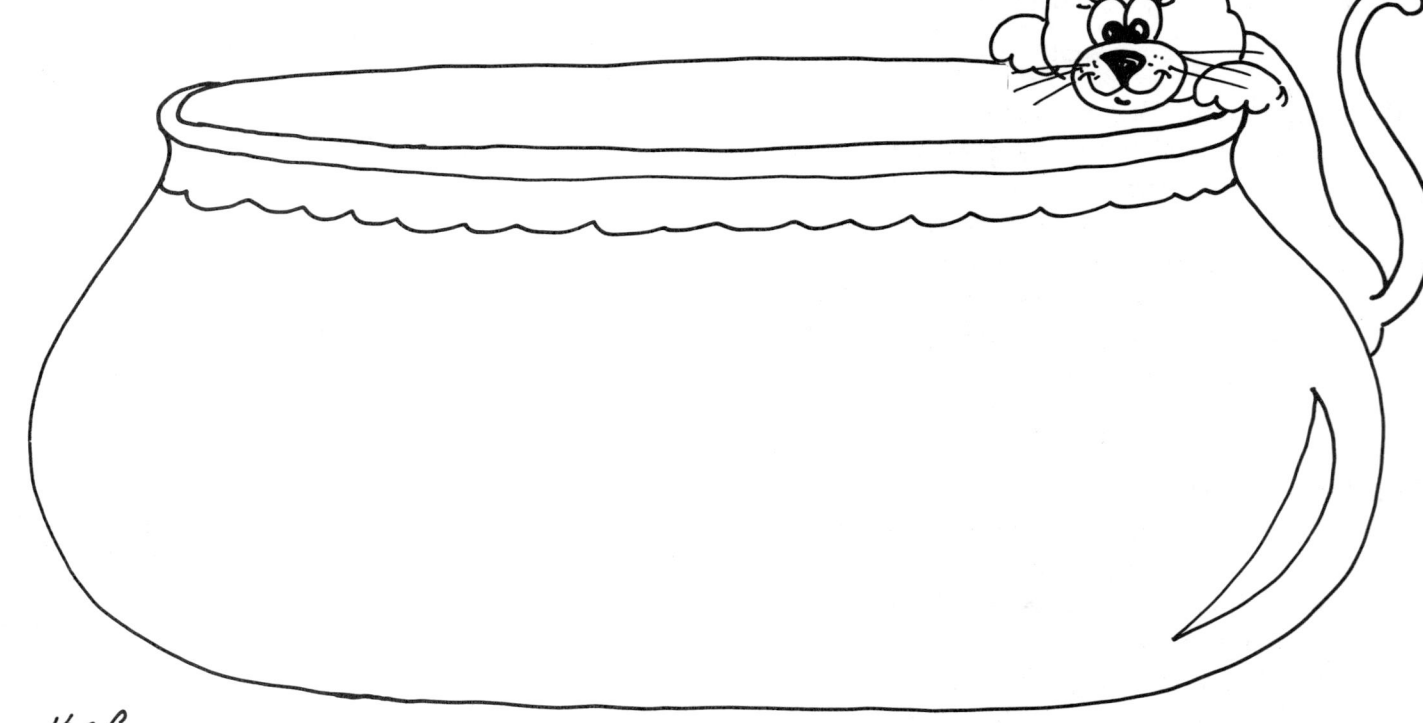

# of differences
[ ]

How are the pictures alike? _____

How are they different? _____

CRITTERS ©1989 AIMS Education Foundation

FISHING FOR FINS

I. Topic Area
Fish anatomy

II. Introductory Statement
Students will construct a goldfish model that shows all its fins and simulates its breathing.

III. Math Skills   Science Processes
- a. Observing
- b. Classifying

IV. Materials
activity sheets
crayons
scissors
live goldfish for observation
tape or glue

V. Key Question
How does a fish swim and breathe under water?

VI. Background Information
Fish breathe by taking dissolved oxygen from water. Fish gulp water through their mouths and pump it over their gills. Most fish have four pairs of gills covered by the operculum. The gills absorb oxygen from the water and replace it with carbon dioxide. Fins are movable structures that help a fish swim and keep its balance. The fins found on the top, underside, and tail (the dorsal, anal, and caudal) help the fish remain upright. The caudal fin propels the fish through the water. The pectoral and pelvic fins are located just behind the gills (with the pectoral fins on top) and are used to turn and stop. The lateral line runs the length of the body and plays an important role for fish as a sensing organ. Fish have no external ears and the lateral line, which has delicate nerve endings all along its length, senses vibrations and movement in the water, thus allowing the fish to "hear."

VII. Management Suggestions
Use the activity sheet to make a working model of the fish, for demonstration purposes, before beginning the activity.

VIII. Procedure
1. Have students observe a goldfish for 5-10 minutes asking them to locate the various fins.
2. Discuss the function of each fin. (See Background Information)
3. Ask how fish are able to breathe under water.
4. Accept answers and elaborate by using an assembled model as a visual aid.
5. Pass out the activity sheet and have students cut out the water strip and fold the bottom 2/3's of it over along the dotted line. Have them label the empty side of the strip with the formulas H_2O (water) and CO_2 (carbon dioxide). This side represents the water composition after it goes through the gills.
6. Have students assemble their own fish models by gluing or taping the fins and lateral line in the appropriate locations. Students may cut out the fish or cut off the top half of the page at the solid line. Insert the water pull strip through any one of the four gill slits. Pull the strip through the gills to simulate the fish breathing.

IX. Discussion Questions
1. How is this form of breathing different from our own?
2. Think of some other animals that breathe with gills.
3. Why do you have to change your goldfish's water if you have no air pump in your fish bowl?

X. Extended Activities
1. Research fresh water and salt water fish for similarities and differences.
2. Observe isopods or tadpoles to see how they use their gills.

XI. Curriculum Coordinates
Art:
Make fish prints using a fish from the market. Paint or ink the surface of this fish and place blank newsprint over the fish. Press the paper onto the fish with your hand and remove the completed print.

Science:
Compare fish and whale fins.

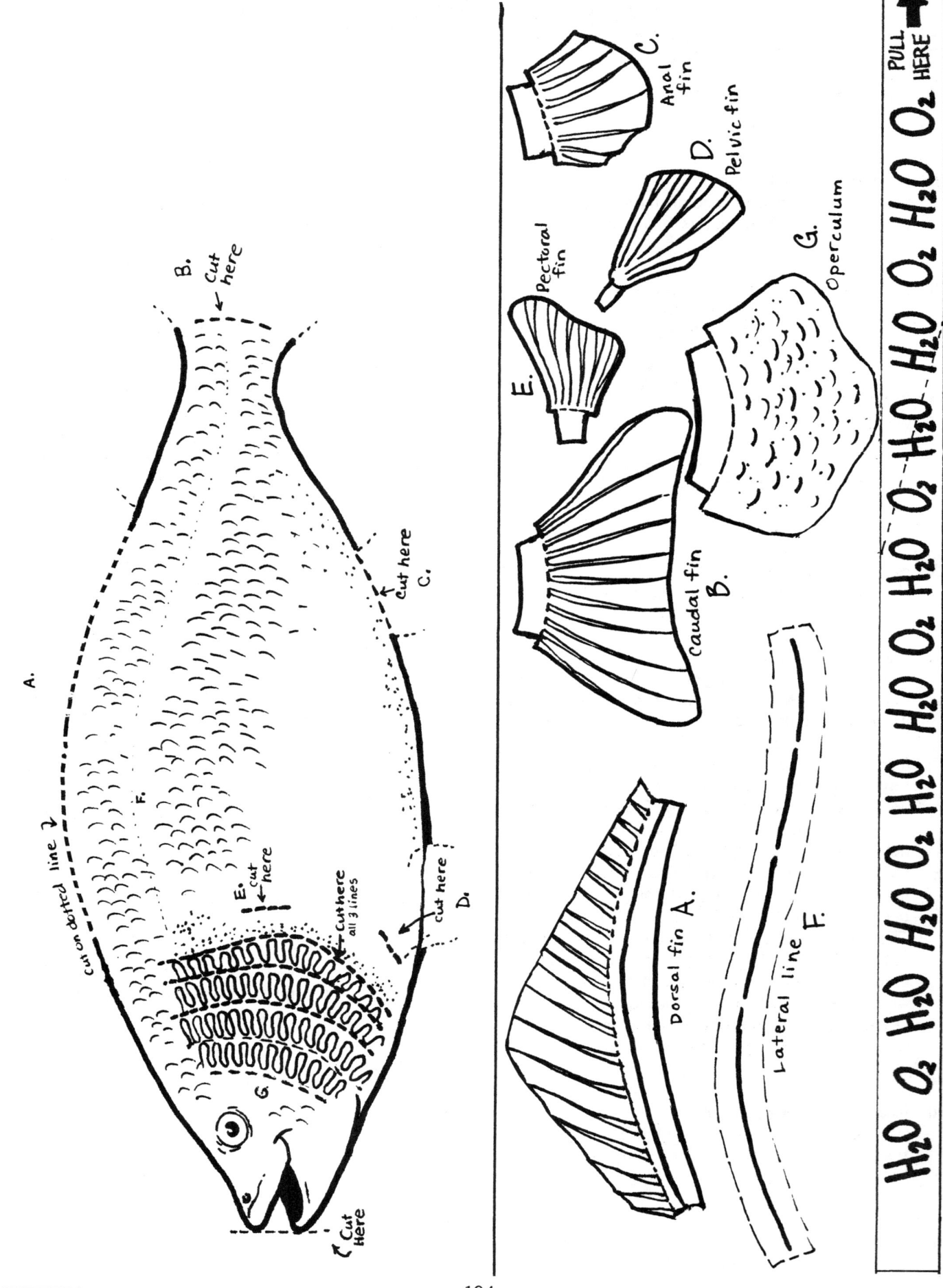

CRITTERS

Randomly place the pieces of the fish puzzle print side up. Each member of the group of four takes a turn placing one piece in position. Each member of the group can move only one piece at a time. A piece that one person has put in place may be moved by another player. This is counted as a move. Talking is not allowed until the puzzle is complete. Play progresses in a clockwise manner. A player may pass if he cannot put a piece in place.

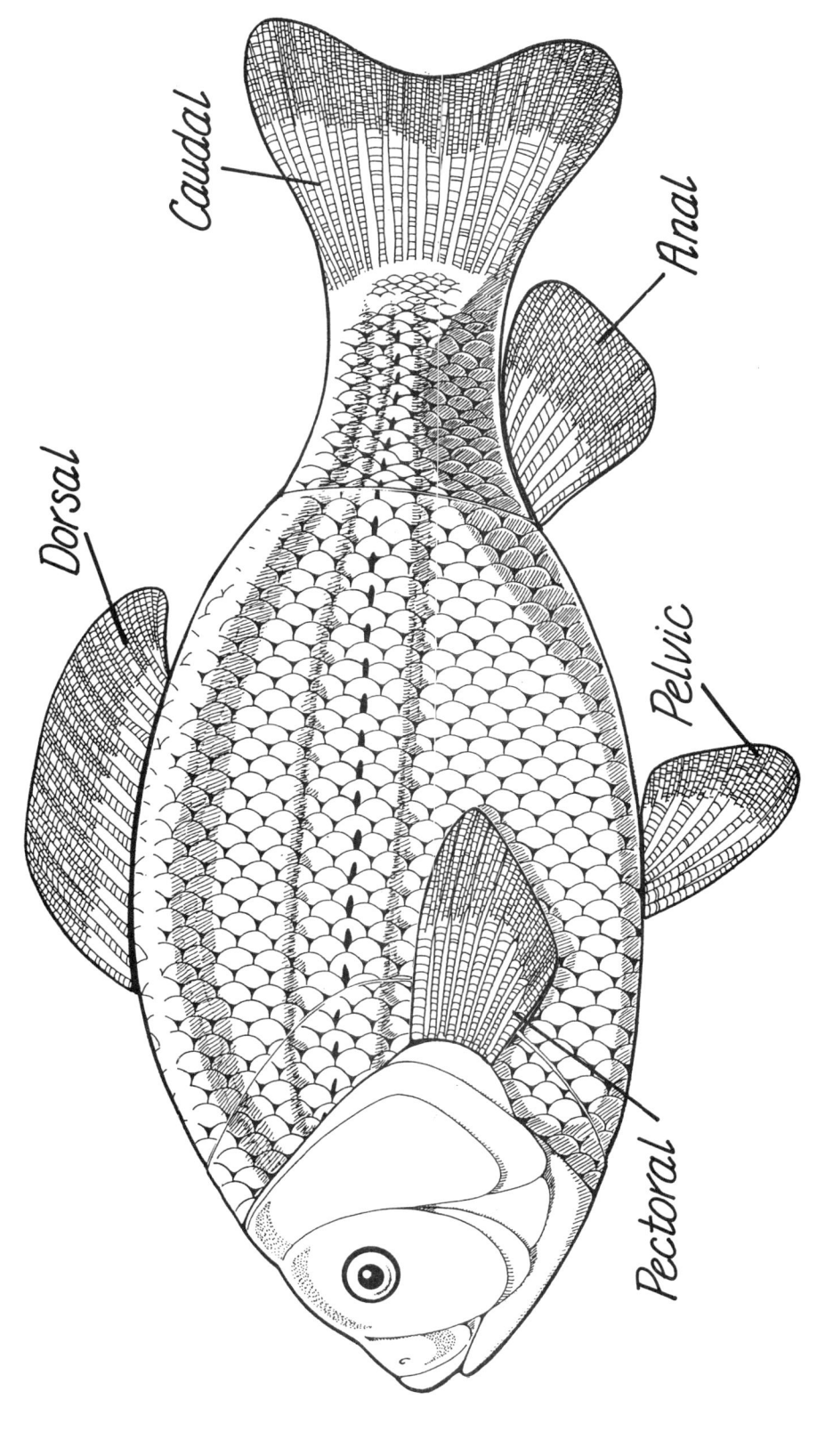

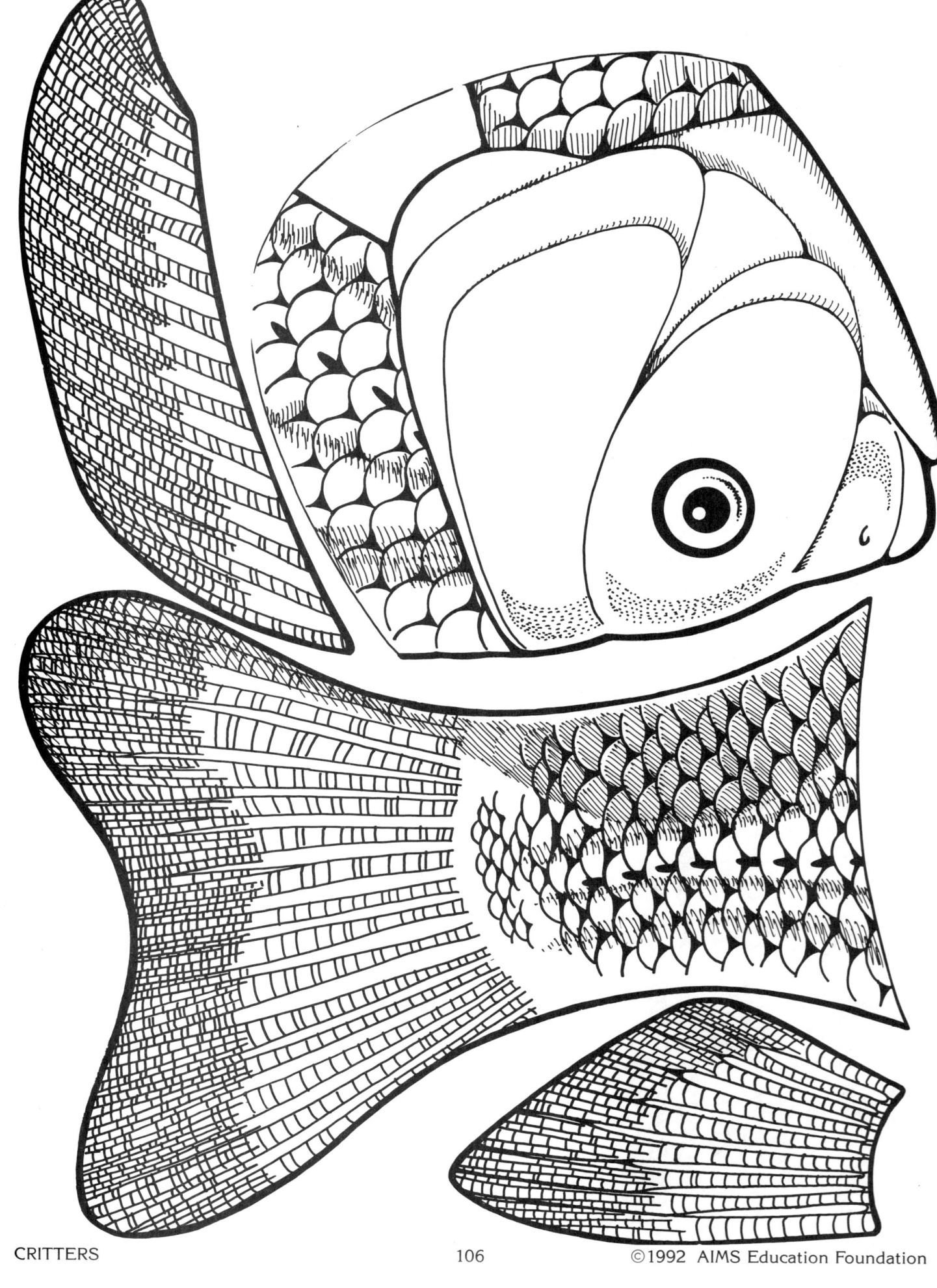

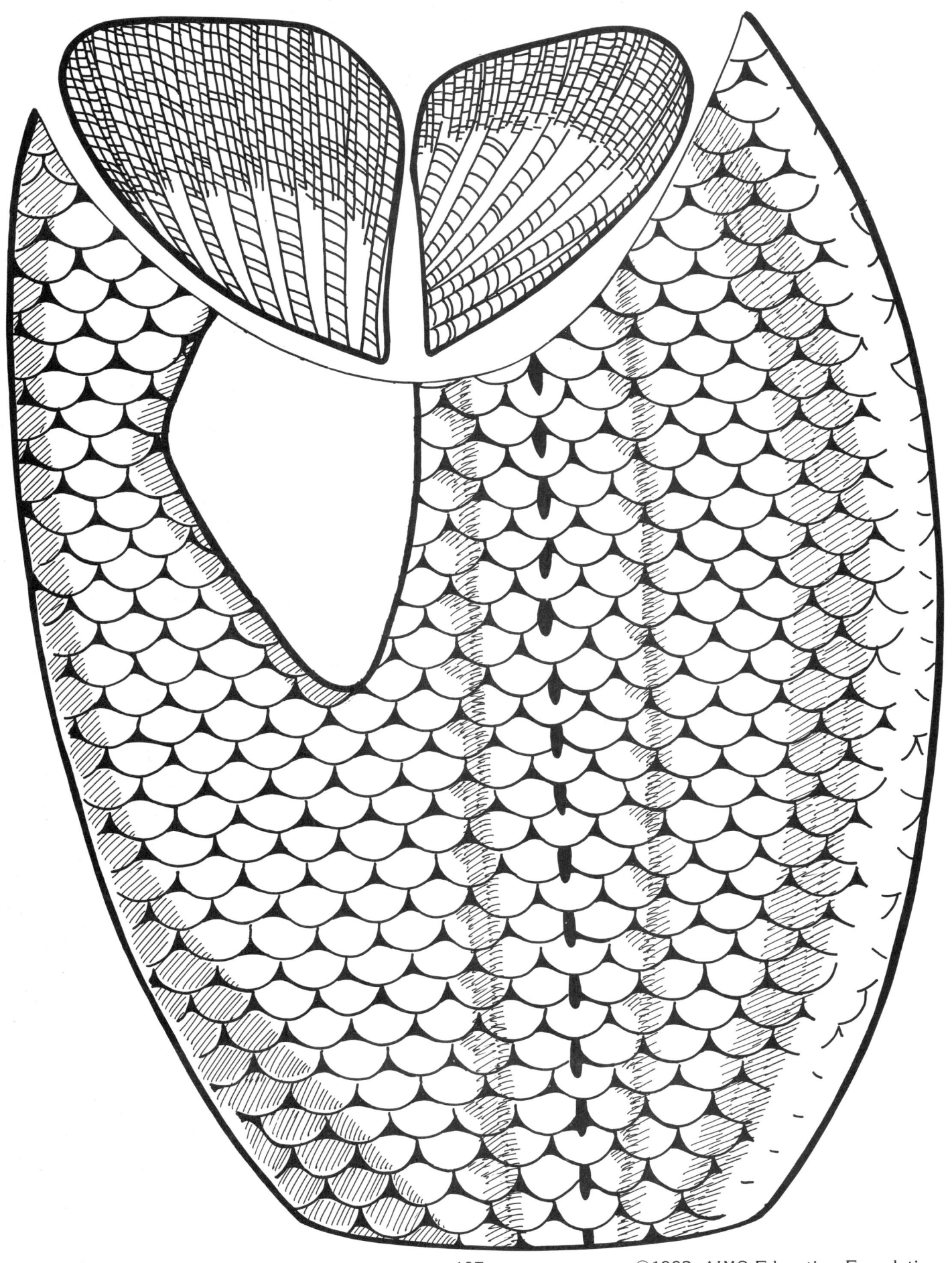

BRINE SHRIMP

I. **Topic Area**
   Brine shrimp

II. **Introductory Statement**
   Students will observe and study brine shrimp as they hatch and grow.

III. **Math Skills** **Science Processes**
   a. Observing
   b. Collecting & recording data
   c. Generalizing

IV. **Materials**
   brine shrimp kit
   glass jars
   activity sheets
   hand lenses
   glass eyedroppers

V. **Key Question**
   How will brine shrimp grow and change over a period of several weeks?

VI. **Background Information**
   See the brine shrimp booklet. The brine shrimp kit also has information.

VII. **Management Suggestions**
   1. Brine shrimp eggs and the instructions and materials needed to hatch them are available in most pet stores in inexpensive kit form. Most kits contain three packages; one containing the eggs, one containing the salt mixture to be added to water, and a package of food.
   2. Students can work in groups on this activity.
   3. Gather enough jars beforehand so that each group has at least one. Large baby food jars or jam jars work well.
   4. Students will be doing this activity for a short time every three days for a period of several weeks.
   5. Prepare the brine solution from the kit according to the directions enclosed. The solution should be made before doing this lesson with students. If you mix your own saline solution, *do not* use iodized salt.
   6. Not all eggs will hatch, so each group should be given 10-15 eggs. The eggs hatch quite quickly once placed in the brine solution.
   7. The glass eyedroppers can be used to catch one or two brine shrimp from the jar for closer observation. Hand lenses also make observing the tiny shrimp easier.
   8. The second activity sheet is designed to be made into a flip book. The dot on each one of the jars is there to serve as a reference point for the student drawings.
   9. The students may want to cut up the second activity sheet and staple it into a flip book before starting their observations and drawings.

VIII. **Procedure**
   1. Fill the jars with brine solution and pass one out to each group.
   2. Have each group count out 10-15 eggs and place them in their jar.
   3. Pass out the first activity sheet and make the brine shrimp booklet by folding the sheet in half and then in half again. Read and discuss the booklet together as a class.
   4. Pass out the second activity sheet. Have students draw a picture of the brine shrimp egg next to the dot in the first jar.
   5. Explain that a picture will be drawn every three days showing the growth of the brine shrimp.
   6. When the brine shrimp eggs hatch have students use the eyedroppers and hand lenses to examine them closely and draw a picture in the next bottle on the activity sheet. The dots on the jars drawn on the activity sheet are to be used as reference points for drawing pictures of the shrimp. The shrimp should be drawn in the same place relative to the dot each day. For example, the student might choose to have the dot represent a point on the top of the brine shrimp's head and draw a picture each day underneath the dot. Older students should be challenged to draw the pictures as accurately as possible so that the growth and changes can be evidenced through the series of pictures.
   7. Older students should attempt to keep an accurate record of the shrimp's growth on the back of the activity sheet detailing length in millimeters, color, swimming methods, etc.
   8. Students will continue the observations for a period of 3-6 weeks.
   9. The activity sheet can be cut apart when it is completed and the pictures stapled in sequence to make a flip book of the shrimp's growth.

IX. **Discussion Questions**
   1. How fast did your brine shrimp grow?
   2. What things did you observe as your brine shrimp grew?
   3. Can you see important organs and body parts in your brine shrimp?
   4. Can you tell the difference between male and female brine shrimp?
   5. Did you observe the skins shed by the brine shrimp?

X. **Extended Activities**
   1. Use an eyedropper to catch a brine shrimp and put it on a slide. With a low power microscope, observe your brine shrimp more closely.
   2. Keep a classroom jar of brine shrimp and study their life cycle for a longer period of time.
   3. Keep track of the number of eggs put in the brine solution and the number of shrimp that actually hatch.
   4. Test your brine shrimp's reaction to changes in light, temperature or salinity.

Brine shrimp grow to be about 12 mm (½") long. They have 10 to 30 pairs of "swimming limbs" that beat 150 to 205 times per minute.

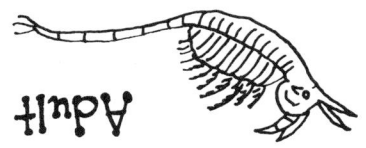

Adult

The swimming limbs point upward because they are sensitive to the light. These limbs are used to filter food particles from the water.

When Brine shrimp hatch, they are the size of a period ".". They double in size in one day.

Brine shrimp do not have any bones. Their outer covering is their skeleton. To grow, they cast off their skeleton and grow a new, larger one. They do this about 12 times until they reach adulthood.

Larva

The female Brine shrimp are larger. Their egg sac is at the point where the body and tail meet. Eggs can be laid every 4-5 days, depending upon the food supply. Dried eggs can be saved in a cool place for long periods of time.

Egg Pouch

BRINE SHRIMP

Brine shrimp are tiny crustaceans that live in salty lakes and along a few coastal areas around the world. They are related to crabs, lobsters and water fleas.

They eat saltwater algae and bacteria. Brine shrimp are used as food for small aquarium animals.

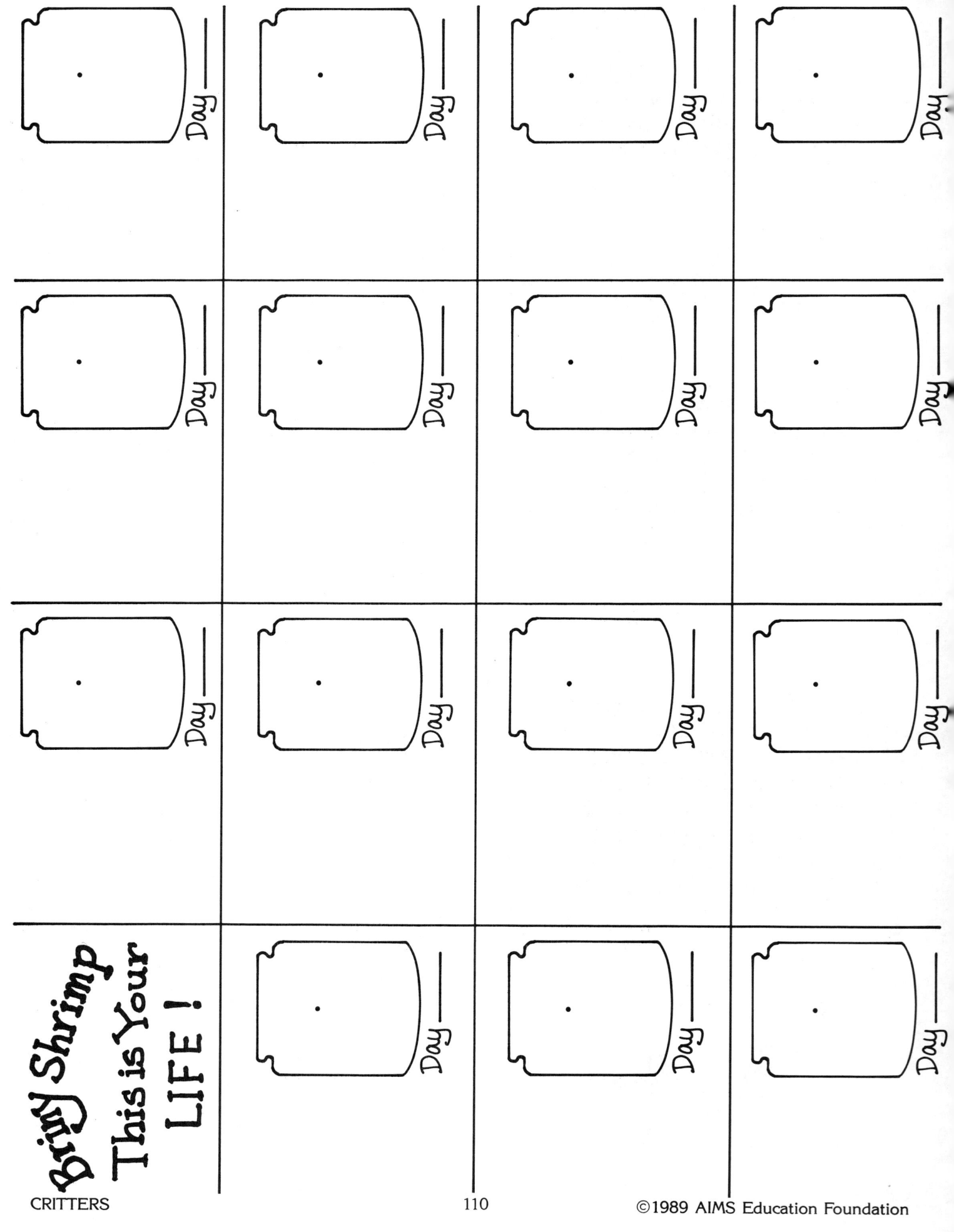

TABLE MANNERS

I. Topic Area
Insect mouthparts

II. Introductory Statement
Students will simulate food gathering with four different types of insect mouths.

III. Math Skills
a. Measuring
b. Graphing

Science Processes
a. Observing
b. Predicting
c. Collecting data
d. Classifying

IV. Materials
Per group of 4:
Mouthparts: 1 flex straw, 1 regular straw with one end cut diagonally to form a point, 1 clothespin, 1 clothespin attached to a small piece of sponge about 1" x 1"
Food sources: paper torn and crumpled into small pieces, 1 narrow necked bottle containing water, 1 cup containing water and covered with a paper towel or plastic wrap taped securely over its opening, 1 tuna can or small bowl containing water
Collection apparatus: 4 plastic or paper cups
Measuring devices: graduated cylinders or measuring cups (optional)

V. Key Question
How are insects adapted to eating certain types of food?

VI. Background Information
An adaptation is any characteristic that helps an organism survive. The adaptation may be in the organism's physical appearance, the way its body functions or the way it behaves. These changes occur through interaction with living and non-living things in the environment. An insect's mouthparts are a set of structures used for eating. They surround the insect's mouth. There are two basic types of insect mouths and mouthparts, those adapted for chewing and those adapted for sucking. Many insects have variations or combinations of the two basic types of mouths. For example, the mosquito has a piercing-sucking mouth, a housefly has a sponging mouth and wasps and bees have chewing-lapping mouths. Chewing insects have two grinding jaws called *mandibles*. They move sideways and are lined with teeth in most species. The jaws are also used for cutting or tearing off food. They have a second pair of less powerful jaws, called *maxillae*, behind the mandibles that are used to push the food down the throat. They also have two lips or flaps that hang down over the mouthparts and cover the front of the mouth. The upper lip is called the *labrum* and the lower lip, the *labium*. Some examples of chewing insects are grasshoppers, crickets, beetles, cockroaches, and termites. Sucking insects have mouthparts adapted from the basic chewing mouth structure to suit their feeding habits. The labium in some insects has become a long, grooved beak with four slender, sharp needles called *stylets*. Stylets are used for piercing and then sucking up juices or blood. In butterflies and moths, the mandibles have lengthened forming a long drinking tube called a *proboscis*. This tube coils up when the insect is not using it to gather liquids. The mandibles in horseflies have become curved swords that can slash an animal's skin and its maxillae have developed into sharp-pointed rods that can penetrate and extract fluids from the skin.

VII. Management Suggestions
1. This activity can be done in one of two ways. The first activity sheet has students simulating the different types of insect mouthparts and how they work. It is a good activity to do by itself and is appropriate for primary students. It could also be done as an introductory lesson for the second activity sheet. The second activity sheet allows students to do some measuring and graphing. The set up for each lesson is identical except for the inclusion of measuring cups or graduated cylinders in the second activity to quantify the amount of food collected by the mouthparts.
2. This activity is designed to be done in groups of four.
3. Prepare the materials for each group ahead of time. Each group will need the materials listed above.
4. To make management easier, each student should pick one food source and collecting cup to keep for the entire activity. Each student will then use each of the four mouth parts, in turn, to try and collect his "food." It will become obvious that not all the mouth parts work well with all the food sources. For example, the chewing mouth (clothespin) will not work well on anything but the bits of paper, while the straws will not be able to collect the bits of paper. It is important for the students to discuss their experiences with each of the four mouthparts and come to a group consensus as to which mouth is adapted best to each food supply.

III. Procedure

1. Discuss differences between insects. Focus on methods of eating, different types of mouthparts and various types of food sources.
2. Discuss how different insects have adapted or changed over time to meet environmental changes, food sources, etc.
3. Discuss the different types of mouthparts on various insects that students may have observed.
4. Pass out the first activity sheet. Show each type of mouth and discuss how it works. Show the students the four kinds of food sources.
5. Using a cup of water, demonstrate how to capture liquid in a straw with your finger. **Note:** Caution students not to use their mouths to suck up liquid in the straw. To capture liquid in the straw, lower it into the liquid and place your finger on top of the straw, trapping the liquid inside. To release the liquid, lower the straw into a "collecting cup" and remove your finger from the top of straw, releasing the liquid. Explain that the piercing-sucking mouthpart (the pointed straw) is the only one that should be used to break through the paper towel or plastic wrap on the covered cup.
6. Pass out a small collecting cup to each student to collect the food gathered by each mouthpart.
7. All students will use all four mouthparts during the lesson, but keep the same collecting cup and food supply.
8. Discuss the activity sheet and have students fill in their predictions as to which mouth is best suited to each food supply. Explain the mechanics of the lesson. Each "feeding period" should be about two minutes.
9. After students have tried each of the four mouth parts to collect their food they need to discuss their observations and come to a group consensus as to which mouth is best adapted to each food source. The students can then fill in the rest of the activity sheet from their observations.
10. The activity can be repeated at a later time using the second activity sheet and having the students count and measure the amounts of each food that the mouthparts collect.

IX. Discussion Questions

1. How does an insect's mouth affect its choice of food?
2. What would happen if all insects had the same type of mouthparts?
3. Where would you look for an insect that had a "sucking" type of mouth? Chewing? Piercing/Sucking? Lapping?

X. Extended Activities

1. Make a list of insects that have each type of mouthpart. Which is the most common type?
2. Discuss how mouthparts relate to where an insect lives.
3. Look up insects in the encyclopedia and draw and label the different types of mouthparts.
4. Design insect mouthparts that would be good at collecting a common food item, such as sugar or fruit.

XI. Curriculum Coordinates

Science:
What kinds of adaptations for eating do mammals have? What about reptiles, birds, amphibians and fish?

Math:
Test each mouthpart again allowing a feeding period that is twice as long. Did you eat twice as much?

Geography:
Identify as many insects in your area as possible. Are there more insects with one particular kind of mouth? Identify the food source for each insect.

Table Manners

Question: How are insects adapted to eating certain types of food?

Food Sources

A. 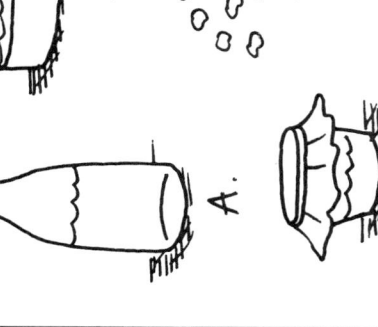 (bottle)
B. (bread/sandwich)
C. (pie)
D. 6 pieces of paper

Mouthpart:

Mouthpart	Best Food Source Prediction	Best Food Source Actual
1. Chewing:		
2. Sucking:		
3. Piercing/Sucking:		
4. Sponging/Lapping:		

Conclusion:

Label each type of mouthpart for the following insects.

1. beetle

2. mosquito

3. butterfly

4. fly

CRITTERS   113   ©1989 AIMS Education Foundation

Table Manners

Question: Which mouthpart of an insect will gather the most food?

Prediction: _____

Mouthpart:	Total Food Eaten:
1. Chewing:	_____ pieces
2. Sucking:	_____ ml
3. Piercing/Sucking:	_____ ml
4. Sponging/Lapping:	_____ ml

Collection Cups: chewing pieces, sucking, piercing/sucking, sponging/lapping

ml of Liquid — sucking | piercing/sucking | sponging/lapping

Pieces — chewing

What do you think?

1. Which mouthpart did you find the easiest to use? Why?
   _____
   _____

2. Which mouthpart was the most difficult to use? Why?
   _____
   _____

CRITTERS

UNDER COVER

I. Topic Area
Animal coverings

II. Introductory Statement
Students will explore the various kinds of animal coverings.

III. Math Skills **Science Processes**
   a. Counting   a. Observing
   b. Graphing   b. Classifying
                     c. Comparing

IV. Materials
soft material to simulate fur or hair collected from pets
feathers
waxed paper
net bag
popsicle sticks
tape and glue
crayons and scissors
activity sheets

V. Key Question
How are animal coverings different?

VI. Background Information
Animals have different kinds of coverings that are an adaptation to their environment. Mammals have hair or fur, birds have feathers, amphibians have smooth skins and scales cover both fish and reptiles.

VII. Management Suggestions
1. Fur can be simulated by small patches of soft, fur-like material or by glueing hair collected from pets or a dog groomer onto small squares of paper.
2. Feathers can be purchased or obtained from a feather pillow.
3. Scales can be simulated by cutting small patches from net produce bags (like the ones used for onions or oranges).
4. Squares of waxed paper simulate smooth skin.
5. In sorting and graphing the small animal pictures there are too many animals with fur to fit on the graph. This is an opportunity for student problem solving or the teacher may wish to eliminate two furry animals before the pictures are given to the students.
6. This activity can be done in one or two sessions.

VIII. Procedure
1. Discuss animal coverings. Then pass out the two activity sheets with the four large animal drawings on them and have the students cut them out.
2. Students color in the animals and glue a patch of the appropriate skin covering on each one.
3. Students tape a popsicle stick to the back of each picture making an animal puppet.
4. Students use the puppets to answer questions about animal coverings. For example, the students would hold up the snake puppet if the teacher showed the class a picture of a fish and asked what kind of skin covering a fish has.
5. After the students have a good grasp of what kind of animals have the various coverings, the activity sheets with the covering graph and the small animal pictures may be passed out.
6. Students glue a sample of each of the coverings in the boxes at the top of the covering graph.
7. Students cut out the small animal pictures and glue them in the appropriate squares on the covering graph.

IX. Discussion Questions
1. Discuss why animals need coverings.
2. Discuss the different kinds of coverings and how they meet the needs of the animals.
3. Discuss other coverings not included in this activity, such as the hard shell of a snail or the thick skin of an elephant.

X. Extended Activities
1. Make "feely" bags that simulate the different textures of animal coverings.
2. Children can bring in toy animals to sort according to covering types or to make a class "zoo."

XI. Curriculum Coordinates
Language Arts:
Brainstorm furry things, then write and illustrate "furry" stories or poems.

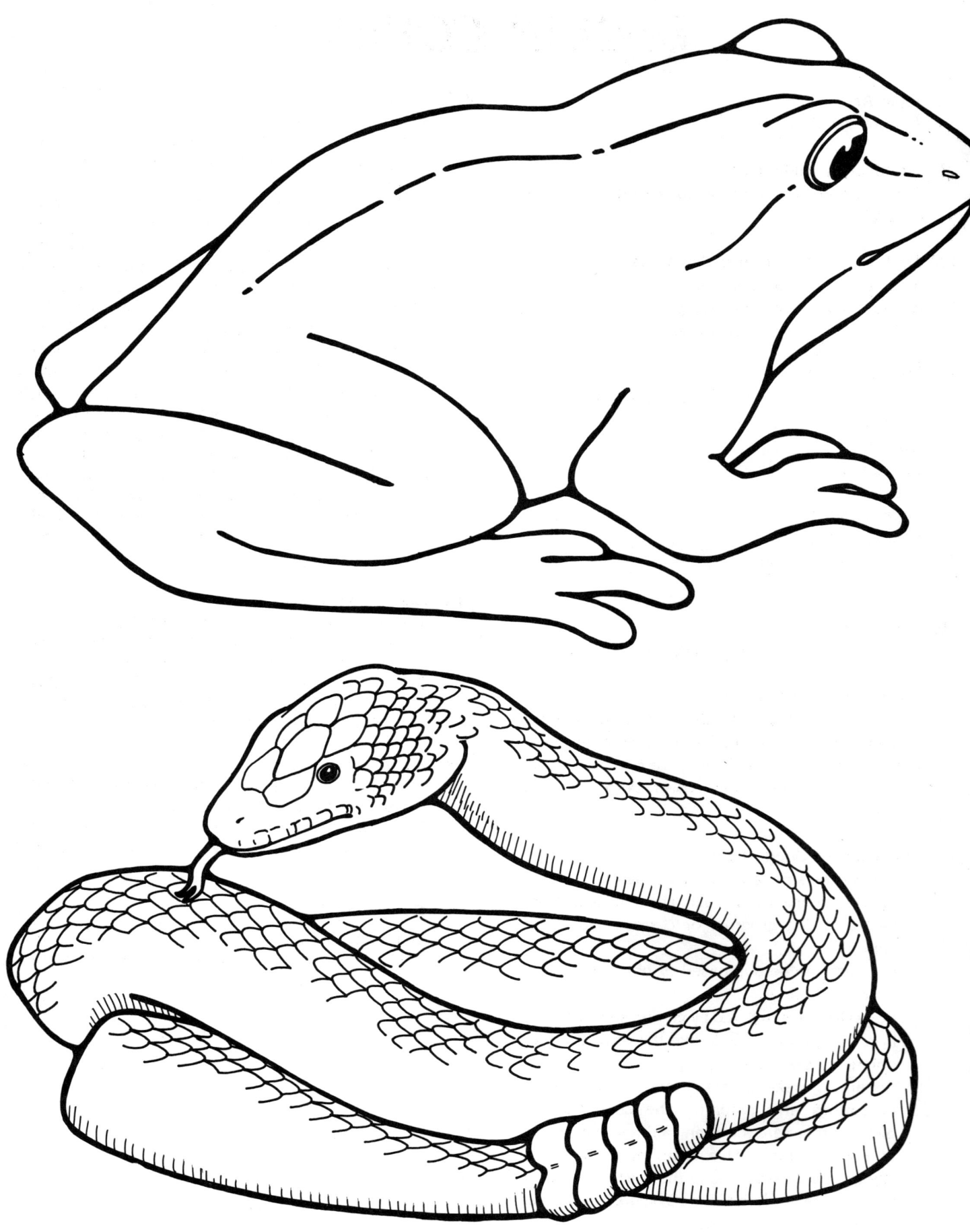

UNDER COVER

Name _____

Fur	Feathers	Scales	Smooth Skin

Name _____

UNDER COVER

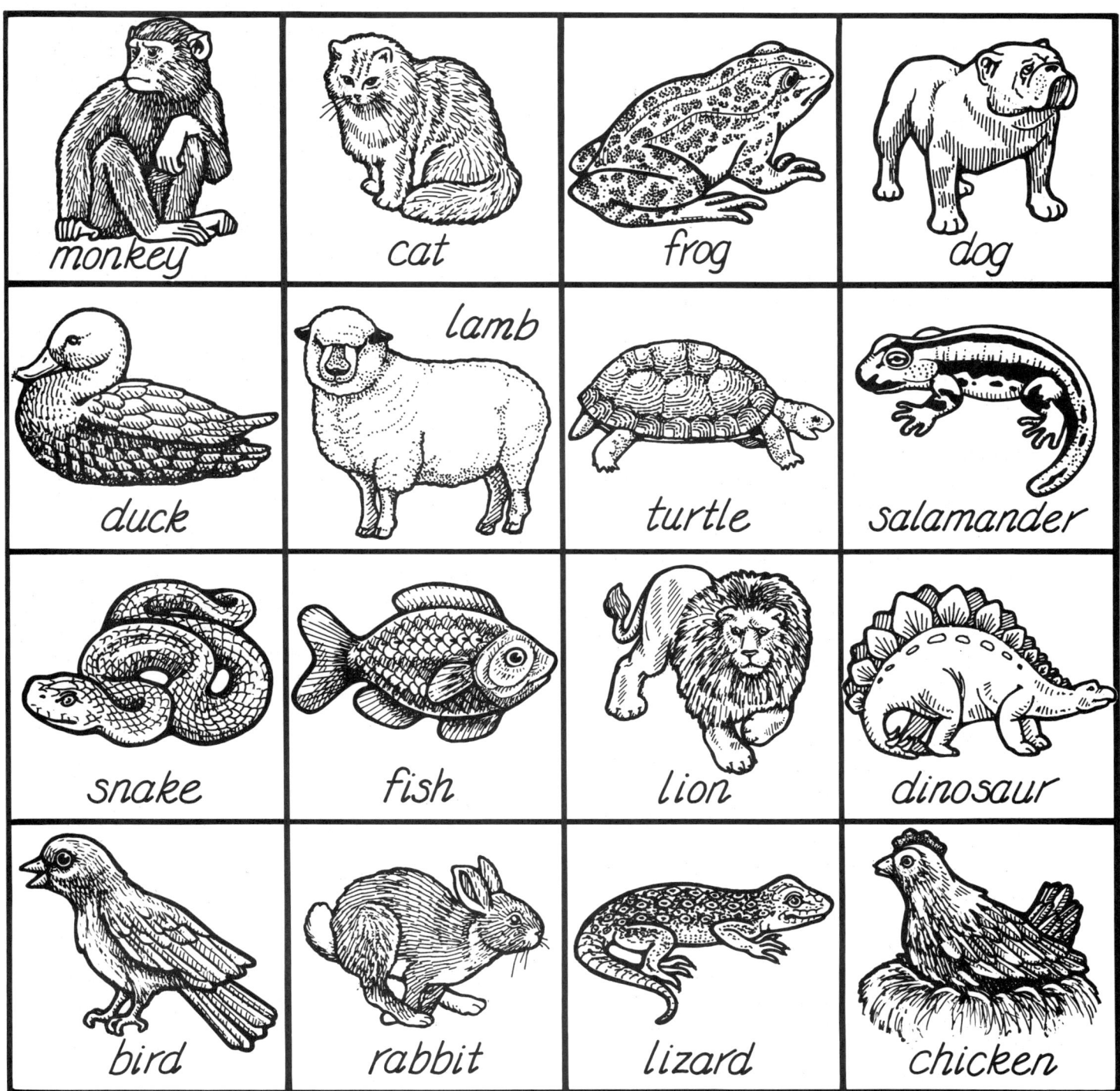

CRITTERS

HIDE AND SEEK

I. Topic Area
Camouflage

II. Introductory Statement
Students will make a critter and see the effects of camouflage on animal visibility.

III. Math Skills
a. Whole number operations
b. Fractions
c. Measurement

Science Processes
a. Predicting
b. Observing

IV. Materials
paint
markers
toothpicks
a variety of objects to build a critter
i.e. egg cartons, paper bags, marshmallows, etc.

V. Key Question
How does camouflage affect a critters ability to survive?

VI. Background Information
Animals use camouflage to protect themselves from predators. Color and body shape are two important variables that enable an animal to blend into its environment. Animals have adapted to the predominate colors in their surroundings. An animal's body shape and size affects its ability to blend into the environment. The patterns of colors on the body covering also affect the animals chances of being seen.

VII. Management Suggestions
1. Be sure to chose beforehand the area where the students can hide their critters. This activity works best if the chosen area is not too large and has definite boundaries.
2. Emphasize that students may not bury the critters.
3. Use tempura paint, markers, or other materials for camouflage.
4. For the critter bodies use paper bags, marshmallows, cardboard egg carton parts, or wads of paper glued or taped together. Toothpicks or sticks can be used for arms and legs.
5. The drawings on the activity sheets include camouflaged critters. Students can locate the critters and color them appropriately.

VIII. Procedure
1. Discuss the key question and activity sheet. Note that the activity sheet is in outline form and is intended to integrate science and language arts.
2. Send students outside to select and observe an environment for their critter within the area chosen for this activity.
3. Record environment information on activity sheet.
4. Keeping environmental information in mind, students create and camouflage a critter from available materials.
5. Record the vital statistics and critter facts on the activity sheet.
6. Have students draw a picture of their critter.
7. Go outside to place critters in their environment. DO NOT BURY CRITTERS!
8. Have students make predictions on the second activity sheet.
9. In small groups students (predators) try to find each others critters. Allow the predators to make one or two sweeps of the area. Set a time limit of a few minutes. The students may enjoy having their teacher be the predator.
10. Students complete activity sheets.
11. Collect all the critters and divide them into two groups making a real graph showing critters found and critters not found.

IX. Discussion Questions
1. Why were you able to locate the critters?
2. Look at the critters in the two groups. What do the critters that were found have in common?
3. What do the critters that were not found have in common?
4. If we were to do this again, how would you change your critter?

X. Extensions
1. Emphasize the use of shapes for camouflage. Use green and brown construction paper.
2. Select a different environment or season and adapt your critter.

XI. Curriculum Coordinates
1. Science: Research animals that use camouflage.
2. Language Arts: Use the "How to Hide A Butterfly" book by Ruth Heller, Grosset and Dunlap Putnam Publishing Group; ISBN 0-148-10478-4.
3. Math: Change fractions to decimals then percentages (see critter fractions activity sheet).

NAME: _____

PREDICTIONS:

How many critters will be found? _____

How many critters will not be found? _____

DATA:

# of critters hidden	# of critters found	# of critters not found
_____	_____	_____

FRACTIONS:

Write a fraction to describe the number of critters found and not found.

$$\frac{B}{A} = \frac{\#\,found}{\#\,hidden} = _____$$

$$\frac{C}{A} = \frac{\#\,not\,found}{\#\,hidden} = _____$$

CRITTER FRACTIONS

Name _____

critters found	total critters	fraction found	lowest terms
8	12		
14	20		
4	16		
20	36		
6	15		

critters not found	total critters	fraction not found	lowest terms
5	15		
16	24		
9	21		
18	30		
12	24		

CRITTERS ©1989 AIMS Education Foundation

GONE FISHING

I. Topic Area
Camouflage

II. Introductory Statement
Students will use paper fish cutouts to see the effect of camouflage on prey populations.

III. Math Skills
a. Sequencing
b. Fractions
c. Computation
d. Comparing inequalities
e. Graphing

Science Processes
a. Predicting
b. Gathering data
c. Drawing conclusions

IV. Materials
Per group of four:
12 black fish, 12 red, 12 white, 12 blue
watch with second hand
several sheets of blue paper
activity sheets

V. Key Question
How does the color of an animal affect its population?

VI. Background Information
For many creatures, color is an important means of defense. The blending of an animal into its environment is called camouflage. Camouflage is one way an animal adapts to its environment. The snowshoe hare is white during the winter so that it can blend in with the snow. When the snow melts the color of the hare changes to brown so that it blends into the surrounding during the summer months, too. Some animals blend so well into their surroundings that they are undetectable when motionless, like the walking stick and tomato worm.

VII. Management Suggestions
1. The fish need to be cut out prior to doing this activity. Students can use the pattern at the top of the second activity sheet or cut out their own fish pattern.
2. The fish need to be the same size and shape and are cut from black, red, white and blue construction paper. Each group will need 12 of each for the activity.
3. Make a few extra fish in case some get torn during the activity.
4. Small rectangles of paper (2"x1") can be used instead of the fish shapes.
5. This activity should be done before doing "Missing Moths" or "Moth Maps."

VIII. Procedure
1. Distribute the activity sheets.
2. Divide the class into groups of four and make sure each group has the cut out fish and 2 sheets of blue paper.
3. The groups will spread the blue paper on a table to act as the fishing pond. The first "fisherman" will turn his/her back to the pond while the other group members spread the 48 fish evenly over the blue paper.
4. Each fishing period will last exactly 10 seconds. The fisherman may only use one hand to pick up fish from the paper. The collected fish may be put in a cup or held in the other hand. The fisherman must attempt to get as many fish as possible in the 10 seconds.
5. The number of each color fish need to be counted and recorded on the activity sheet.
6. The above procedure will be repeated until all four people have had a chance to fish. Make sure that all the fish are replaced before starting each new fishing period.
7. Have the groups share their data and make a data chart on the board. The activity sheets should be completed and the results graphed and discussed.

IX. Discussion Questions
1. Why were some fish caught more than others?
2. How did your group data compare to the class data?
3. How does this activity relate to animals living in their natural evironment?
4. What would happen to snowshoe hares if there was no snow one winter and the ground stayed brown?

X. Extended Activities
1. Use other colors of fish and backgrounds and repeat the activity.
2. Repeat the activity with the same color, but different size fish, to see if size makes a difference.

XI. Curriculum Coordinates
Language:
Write a story about a brown mouse who lived in a white environment.

Art:
Do a camouflage art lesson in which the students draw pictures with objects hidden in them.

Research:
Find other animals that use camouflage.

Name_____

GONE FISHING

Graphing our class data

Each fish represents ____ fish.

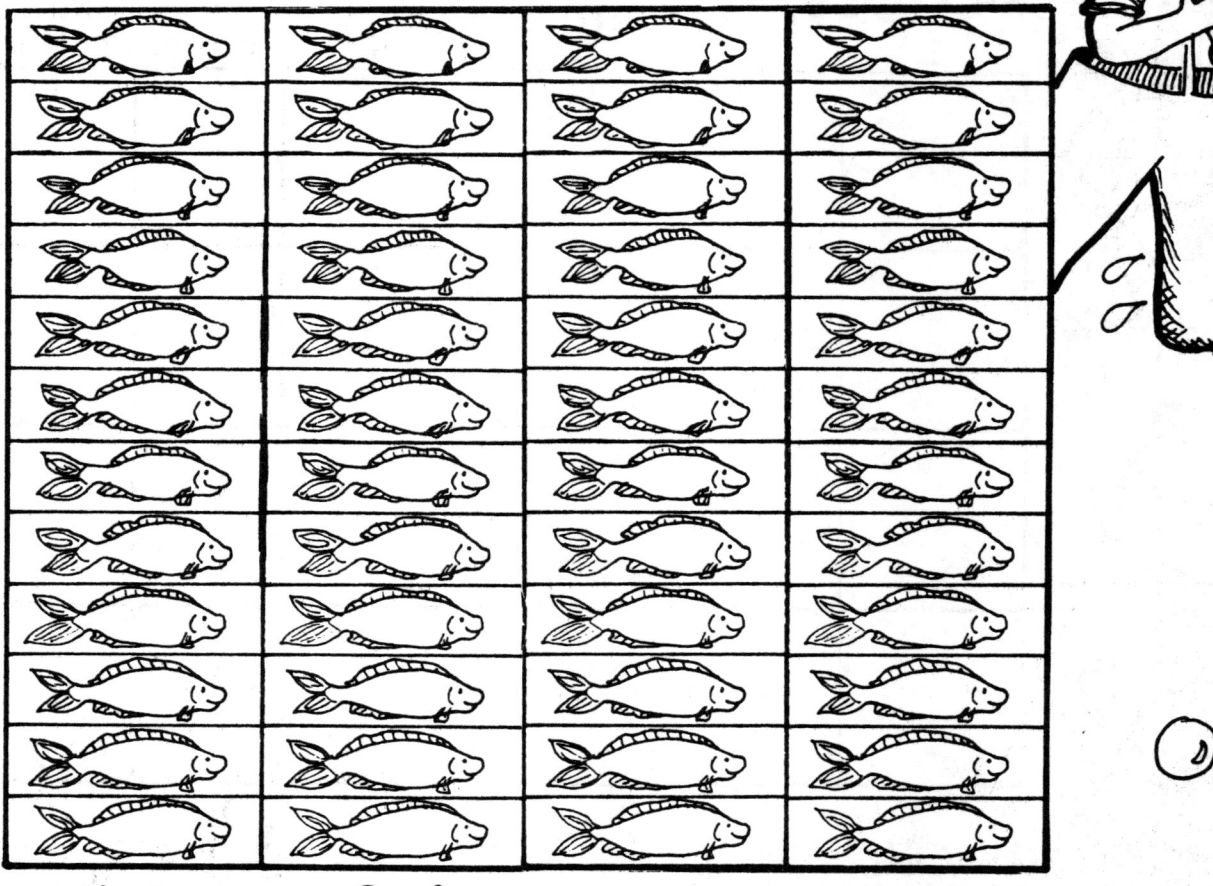

White   Red   Blue   Black

Color of Fish

Drawing Conclusions

CRITTERS   126   ©1989 AIMS Education Foundation

GONE FISHING

Name_____

	Fisherman's Total	Total # of Fish	Fraction Caught	Fraction Not Caught
White		12		
Red		12		
blue		12		
Black		12		

Use >, =, < symbols to record your results.

The fraction of red fish caught is ◯ the fraction of white caught.

The fraction of blue fish caught is ◯ the fraction of black caught.

The fraction of blackfish not caught is ◯ the fraction of red fish not caught.

Now try these... Fill in the blanks.

The fraction of _____ caught is > the fraction of _____ caught.

The fraction of _____ not caught is < the fraction of _____ not caught.

How about this one... Write your own.

_____ ◯ _____.

CRITTERS   127   ©1989 AIMS Education Foundation

MISSING MOTHS

I. **Topic Area**
Camouflage

II. **Introductory Statement**
Students will observe an environment with a variety of moths to see the effects of camouflage on animal visibility.

III. **Math Skills**   **Science Processes**
   a. Estimating   a. Observing
   b. Counting   b. Recording data
   c. Graphing   c. Concluding

IV. **Materials**
brown, white and green construction paper
newspaper want ads
moth pattern
activity sheets
glue and tape
scissors and crayons

V. **Key Question**
How does camouflage affect an animal's ability to be seen?

VI. **Background Information**
An animal's ability to blend into an environment is called camouflage. Camouflage can be used for defensive or offensive purposes. A rabbit uses camouflage to hide from predators. A mountain lion uses it to hide until a prey is close enough to attack. Animals can be camouflaged by both color and shape. A walking stick is an example of this. Its shape and color make it appear to be part of a tree branch. One of the most dramatic cases of an animal's response to a changing environment is the sphinx moth of England. The sphinx moths that lived near Manchester were light colored so that they blended into the light colored bark of the surrounding trees. Prior to 1850 the vast majority of the moths were light colored. By 1894 95% of the sphinx moths were dark colored. This change occurred because of the environmental effects of the industrial revolution. The local industries were burning large amounts of fuel that produced a new phenomenon, air pollution. The vegetation became coated with this pollution and turned darker in color. The light colored moths became highly visible on the darkened trees and were easy targets for their predators. In 1848 the first black moth was captured, and in 47 years successive populations of moths had changed their color to adapt to the darker environment. The darker moths are presently more populous than the lighter ones. However, due to ecological efforts and the use of cleaner fuels, the light colored moth is beginning to make a comeback. This case is unusual because coloration changes generally occur over a much longer period of time. This example clearly illustrates man's impact on the environment.

TIME LINE

Industrial revolution		*Environment improves*	
1800	1850	1900	1950
All moths are light	First dark moth found	Most moths (95%) have become dark	Light moths increasing

VII. **Management Suggestions**
1. Before doing the lesson you must prepare the "moth environment." To do this tape two sheets of want ads together. Be sure the pages are covered with small print. Use the moth pattern next to the title to cut out and randomly glue brown, green, white and newsprint (cut from the want ads) moths onto the two sheets. The numbers of each kind of moth may vary.
2. You may want to cut the newsprint moths out of another identical page of want ads and glue them in the exact position from which they were cut out, making them very well camouflaged.
3. Laminate the sheets if desired.
4. This activity should be done after "Gone Fishing." Doing it before will adversely affect the results of "Gone Fishing."

VIII. **Procedure**
1. Before the students arrive, place the newspaper with the moths glued to it on a wall, bulletin board or chalkboard in the front of the classroom and cover it with a sheet of butcher paper.
2. To begin the lesson tell the class that you have a page of paper moths under the butcher paper. Their task will be to look at the paper for 10–15 seconds and estimate the total number of moths and the number of different kinds (colors) of moths.
3. Pass out the student activity sheet. Tell the students not to color the large cut out moth.
4. Remove the butcher paper and allow students to observe the paper for 10 seconds. Re-cover it with the butcher paper.
5. Have the students complete the first section by recording their estimates of the number of types of moths and the total number of moths they saw. Discuss their estimations.

6. Uncover the paper and count the actual number of types and the total number of moths. Record this data in section two of the activity sheet.
7. Discuss how the predictions and results compared. Because of camouflage, many students may not have seen the newsprint moths. This should be related to how animals depend on camouflage to help them survive.
8. Complete section three by having the students count and record the number of each type of moth.
9. Complete the bar graph by asking the students to raise their hands when you call out the color of the moth that was easiest for them to see. Record this data on the board and have the student color in the graph accordingly.
10. Have the students cut out the moth in the top part of the activity sheet.
11. Tell them that they are going to choose a spot in the room to place (tape) their moth.
12. Each student will select a place and color their moth so that it blends into that location and is camouflaged. Encourage students to consider both the colors and the patterns in the area they choose.
13. The students leave the class and re-enter one at a time and tape their moth to its location.

Note: Moths must be in plain sight and not be placed under anything.

14. All students return and look around to see how many moths they can see.
15. Tell students the story of the sphinx moth from the background information.

IX. Discussion Questions

1. Which moths were the most camouflaged? The least?
2. What would happen if the background had been red? black? white?
3. How does this example relate to animals in a forest?
4. Why are different moths more easily seen by some of our class?
5. Which moths were not found in our classroom? Why?

XI. Curriculum Coordinates

Art:
Use cutouts to make a camouflage collage.

Language:
Write a letter to a brown moth explaining why it would not be a good idea to move to a red plant.

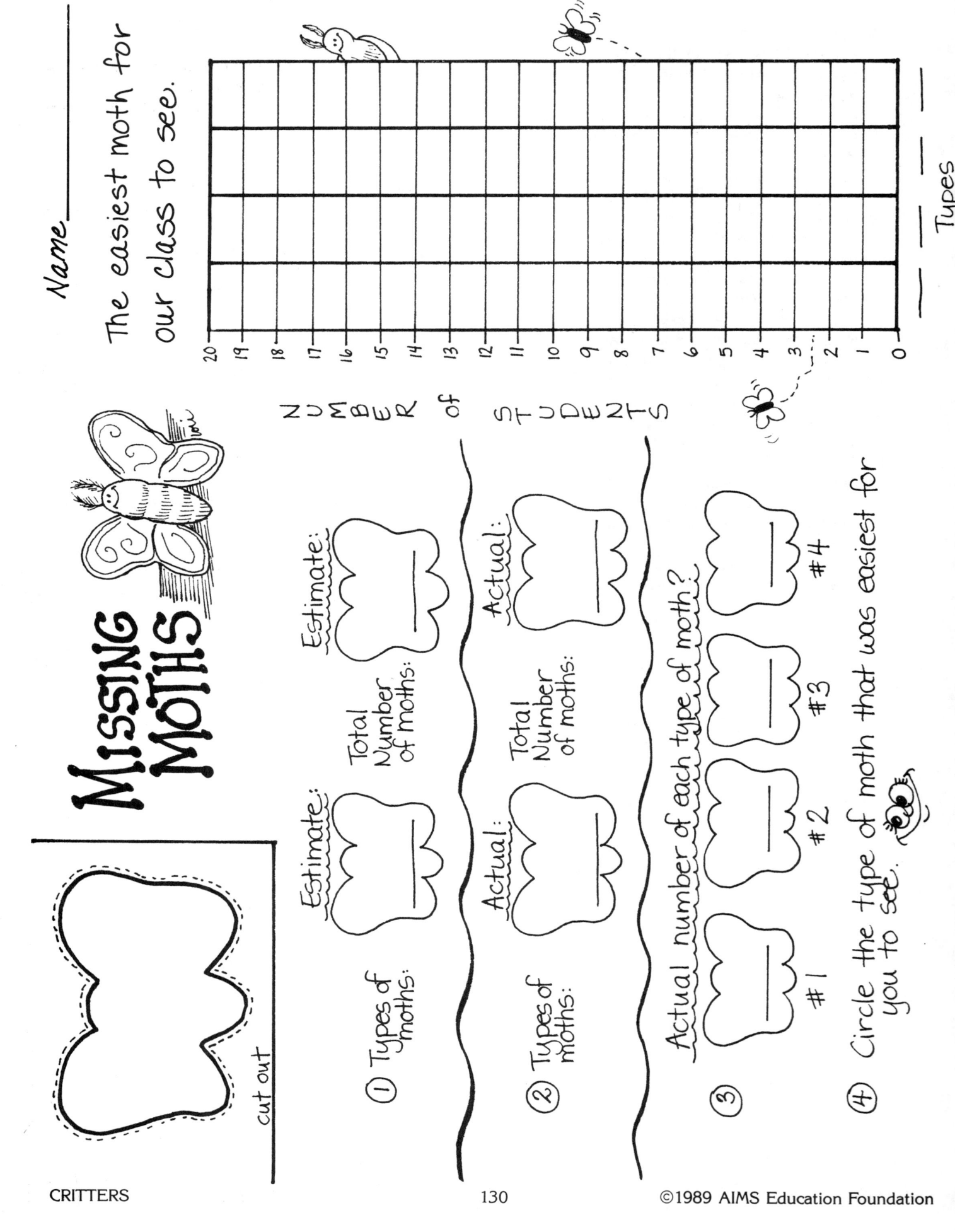

MOTH MAPS

I. Topic Area
Camouflage

II. Introductory Statement
Students will try to locate moths camouflaged on a coordinate grid and map their location.

III. Math Skills
a. Estimating
b. Graphing
c. Coordinate mapping
d. Computing (fractions, decimals, percentages)

Science Processes
a. Observing
b. Collecting & recording data
c. Concluding

IV. Materials
construction paper (brown, white, green, other colors optional)
newspaper want ads
large ruler and marking pen
activity sheets
glue and tape

V. Key Question
How does a moth's color affect its ability to be located on a coordinate map?

VI. Background Information
See background information for "Missing Moths."

VII. Management Suggestions
See management suggestions in "Missing Moths."

VIII. Procedure
1. Make the want ad sheet "moth environment" as described in "Missing Moths." Divide the paper into sixteen coordinate sections as shown on the activity sheet. Use a marker and a meter stick to draw the grid on the want ad sheets.
2. Have the students sit so that they are at least two or three meters from the moth environment.
3. Pass out the activity sheets and discuss. Students are to decide on a key for describing the moths, i.e. Brown = B, Want Ad = W, etc. Note: Five lines are given so that you can increase the number of kinds of moths.
4. Using their key students will map the locations of the moths in the moth environment on the activity sheet grid. Do not allow the students to go near the sheet for a closer look. Tell them to mark all of the moths they see on the grid.
5. Students will complete the "My Record" section by labeling the columns with their codes and recording the coordinates (letter, number) of each moth that was found. Each type of moth has its own column.
6. Ask the students to add the columns and record the total number of each moth that they found. Point out all of the moths to the class and have them record the actual number of each kind.
7. Complete the table and graph on page two with the data from page one and write a conclusion about the effectiveness of camouflage.
8. Discuss these conclusions.

IX. Discussion Questions
1. How did the moth's color affect its ability to be found?
2. Which color was the easiest to locate?
3. Which color was the most difficult to locate?
4. Were there factors other than camouflage that affected your ability to locate each moth?

X. Extended Activities
1. Use different color moths.
2. Make moths from felt instead of paper.
3. Do this activity on the grass in a marked off area using various shades of green moths.

XI. Curriculum Coordinates
Math:
Make a coordinate map of your classroom showing where each desk is located.

Computer:
Move the turtle in LOGO by giving it coordinates and using the set position commands.

Social Studies:
Use a United States map and identify the coordinates of each state capital.

Name _____

Moth Maps

Using the information from the Data Table section of page one, complete the table and graph.

Moth Type	Total Found	Actual Total	Found/Total	Decimal Equivalent	Percent Found

Graph the percent of each type that were found.

Type	0	10	20	30	40	50	60	70	80	90	100

What can you conclude about the effectiveness of camouflage?
_____
_____
_____

CRITTERS

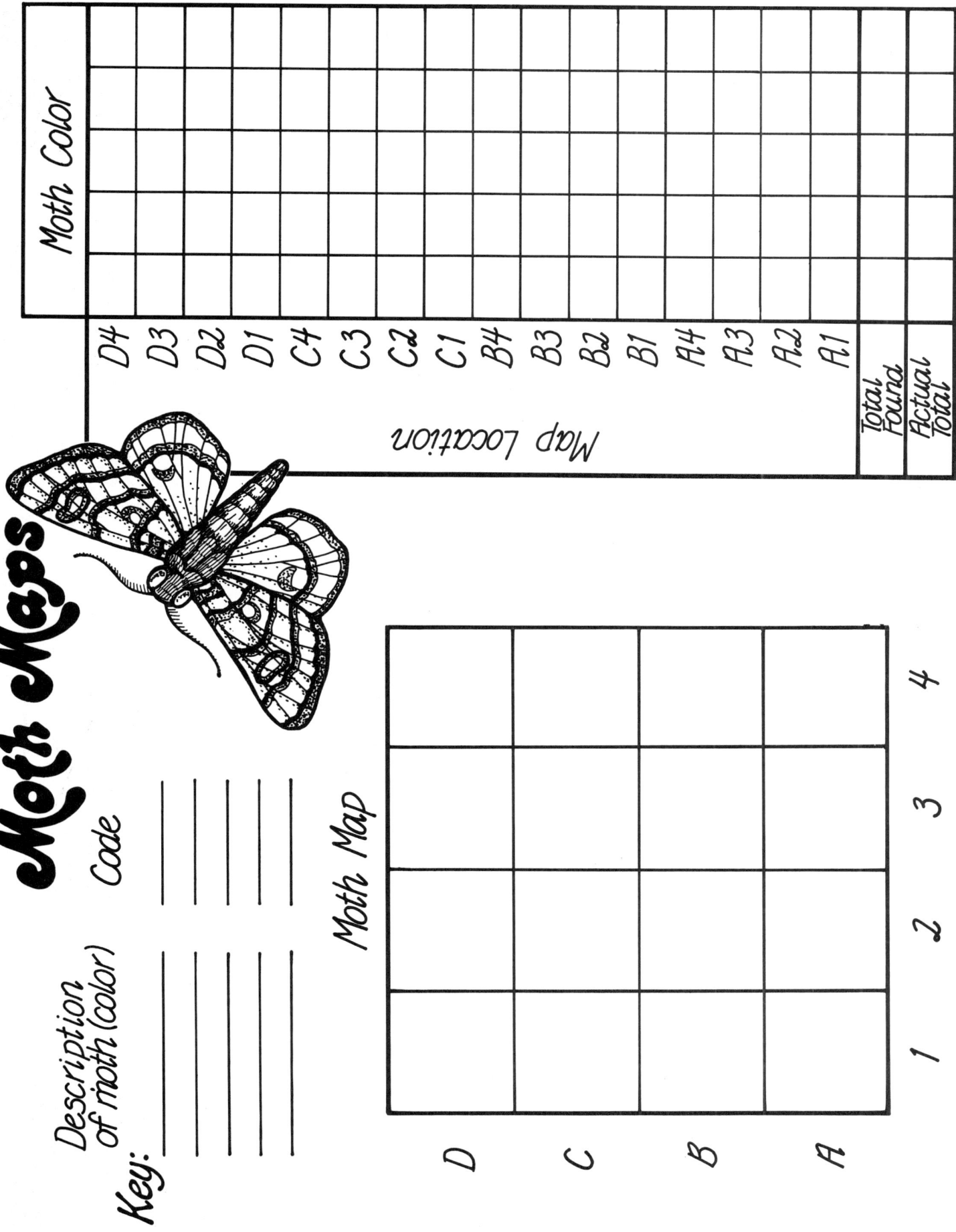

Food Chains

Living things need food to give them energy. A food chain is the path by which energy passes from one living thing to another. Green plants use energy from the sun to make food. Green plants are called producers because they are responsible for making the food that the higher level animals (consumers) eat.

Consumers that only eat plants are called herbivores. (grasshopper) Those that eat only meat are called carnivores, (cat) and those that eat plants or meat are called omnivores. (bear)

A food chain is a simplified way to look at the energy that passes from producers to consumers. A food web is a more realistic way of looking at the relationships of plants and animals in an environment. A food web is created when several food chains are linked together. Predators eat a variety of prey. It is likely that a predator from one food chain would be linked to the prey of a different chain. (hawk) (snake) (mouse) (small bird)

FOOD WEB

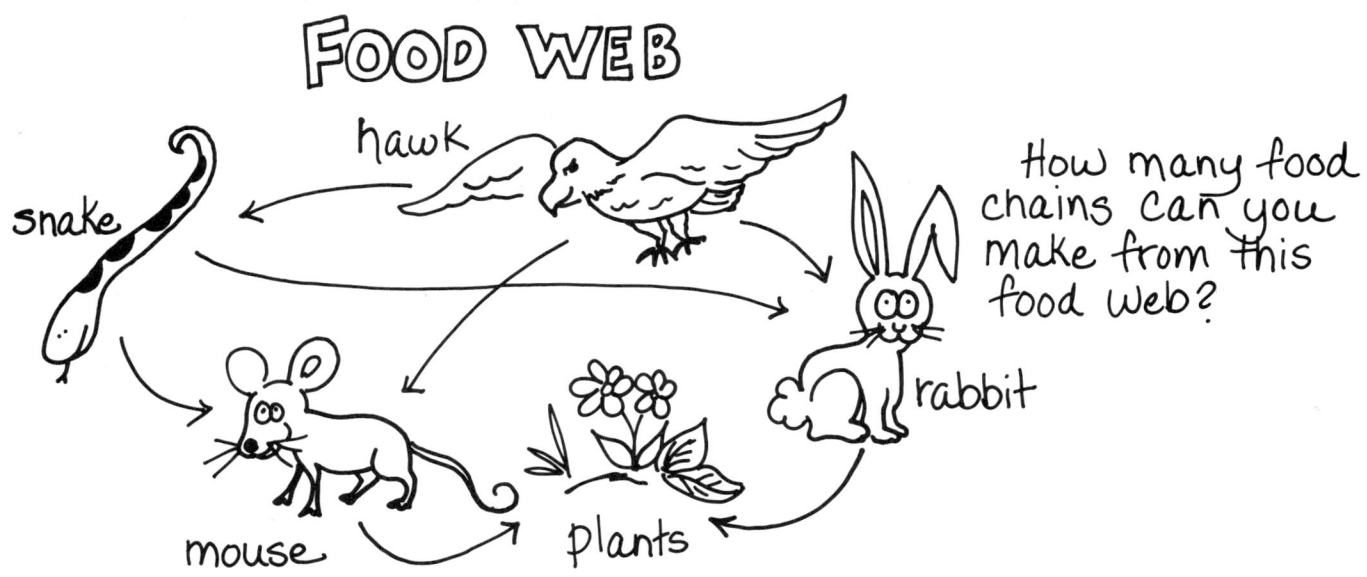

How many food chains can you make from this food web?

Decomposers are an important link in a food chain or web. They are microorganisms that are able to break down large molecules into smaller parts.

Decomposers can be found at any link of a food chain. They return the nutrients that are in a living thing to the soil. Without decomposers, future generations of plants would not have the nutrients they need to grow.

CRITTERS

CATCH ME IF YOU CAN

I. Topic Area
Food chains and predator/prey relationships

II. Introductory Statement
Students will play a tag game to experience the relationships between predators and their prey in a food chain.

III. Math Skills   **Science Processes**
   a. Computation   a. Observing
   b. Area   b. Gathering data
   c. Comparing   c. Generalizing
                     d. Applying

IV. Materials
brown, red and yellow yarn cut into pieces about 40 cm long as follows:
   brown, enough for half the class; red, enough for 1/3 of the class; yellow, 1/3 of the class also
large bag of popped popcorn
sandwich size baggies, 1 per student
Optional — 1 small bag of cheese popcorn for extension activity

V. Key Question
How is energy passed along a food chain from link to link?

VI. Background Information
All foods contain chemical energy. A food chain shows the transfer of energy through the chain. Energy is released from the sun and converted by green plants (producers in the food chain) that use light to make food through photosynthesis. Primary consumers are dependent on green plants, and thus the sun, for food energy. Higher level consumers are dependent on the animals that eat plants or other animals, thus the energy is passed from link to link in the food chain. All links are ultimately dependent on the sun for their food energy. Some energy is lost between each link in a food chain. Because of the energy loss, each higher level has fewer living things than the level below it, thus food chains rarely exceed four links. A pyramid of energy illustrates the energy transfer between predators and prey. Animals at the top of the pyramid are fewer in number and need to eat many smaller animals to get enough energy to survive. The primary consumers that feed on green plants are much more numerous. In a well balanced ecosystem, the producers and consumers at each level have numbers that are large enough to insure their survival without depleting their food supply, thus the pyramid effect with many producers and primary consumers and few of the highest level consumers.

VII. Management Suggestions
1. Find an area with well defined boundaries for this outdoor activity.
2. Stress safety and demonstrate the proper way to tag. Make sure students understand the rules before going outside.
3. Use the activity sheet after the final round of play.

VIII. Procedures
1. Discuss food chains and food webs. Refer to science texts or study prints to illustrate this idea. Discuss predator/prey relationships.
2. Tell the students they are going to play a tag game that will simulate a natural food chain and illustrate a biomass pyramid.
3. Divide the class into 3 even groups. Each group will be assigned a different color of yarn. Pass out the yarn and have each student tie the yarn around his or her wrist in a bow, so that they are easy to remove at the end of the game.
4. The animals the students simulate are represented by the colors of yarn.
   Brown = grasshoppers   Yellow = lizards
        Red = hawks
5. Explain the predator/prey relationships in this chain.
   Hawks hunt only lizards.
   Lizards hunt only grasshoppers
   Grasshoppers eat only grass (which is represented by the popcorn).
6. Pass out a baggie to each student which will be used as a stomach. The students playing grasshoppers will put popcorn gathered from the ground into their baggies. The students playing lizards will try to tag the grasshoppers. If they are successful the grasshopper is "dead" and the contents of its baggie are emptied into the lizards bag (the empty baggie stays with the grasshopper to be used again in the next round). Lizards and hawks may not pick up popcorn from the ground. Hawks may only tag lizards and if successful, get the contents of the lizards' baggies.
7. For the animals to survive, they must not be tagged during the game and their stomachs (baggies) must be filled as follows by the game's end.
   grasshoppers — 1/3 full
   lizards — 2/3 full
   hawks — full
8. Go outdoors and select an area to be the ecosystem. For the first round, the area should be small, so that the students can experience the effects of crowding on animal populations. Students may not leave the area during the game.

CRITTERS ©1989 AIMS Education Foundation

9. Set up two or three safe zones within the area. Animals may not prey on each other in these zones. Select an area for the "dead" animals (those that are tagged) to wait for the next rounds.
10. Spread out a large bag of popped popcorn over the ecosystem.
11. Signal the primary consumers, the grasshoppers, to begin eating grass (gathering popcorn). After 30 seconds allow the lizards to enter the area. After 30 more seconds allow the hawks to enter the ecosystem. Allow the students to play for several minutes or until there are no more prey. At the end of play all remaining animals must have the right amount of food in their baggies, or they too are dead. Note the length of time the game lasted.
12. After round one, ask why the game only lasted a few minutes. Discuss crowding and the number of predators vs. number of prey. Write down the number and kinds of animals that are still alive.
13. The second round can be played in the same area as round one, with the following changes, half the students will play grasshoppers (brown), the other half should be divided so that two-thirds of them are lizards and one-third are hawks. Play the game again. Discuss the effects changing the population numbers had on the time the game lasted.
14. For the third round leave the animal poplations as they were in round two but greatly enlarge the area in which the game is played. Discuss the effects of the larger area on the time the game lasted.
15. Return to the classroom. Use the activity sheet to illustrate the numbers of predators and prey in an ecosystem and to make a biomass mobile. Discuss the energy flow from the producers to the higher level consumers. Emphasize that the energy in a food chain originates from the sun. A biomass pyramid could also be made by centering and gluing the pieces, one on top of another.

IX. Discussion Questions
1. Why did the games end? How long should they last?
2. What numbers of predators and prey worked the best?
3. How does area affect predator/prey relationships?
4. How is this game related to a real ecosystem?
5. Create a food chain and discuss.
6. Where does grass get energy?
7. How is the biomass mobile related to the predator/prey game? Why are green plants so important in a food chain?

X. Extended Activities
1. Mix some cheese popcorn with the large bag. Have it represent a pesticide. Do not point this out to students until the end of the game. An animal with three or more cheese corn kernels in their stomach would have died to toxic poisoning.
2. Create a variety of food chains using other animals.
3. Play the game introducing predator/prey behaviors such as camouflage, hunting techniques, decoying, running speed, freezing and playing dead.

XI. Curriculum Coordinates
Geography:
Research various geographical areas and list several food chains.

Art:
Design a poster illustrating food chains and food webs.

CATCH ME IF YOU CAN...

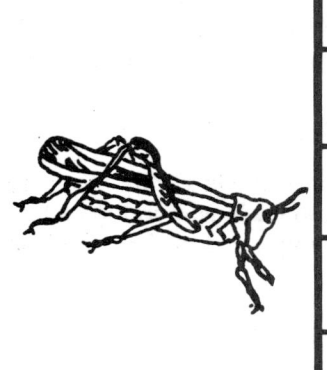

Square	Length	Width	Area
A		x	=
B		x	=
C		x	=
D		x	=

1. Find the area of each square.
2. Imagine that the squares below are part of an ecosystem that includes grass, grasshoppers, lizards and hawks. Think about the numbers of living things in a balanced ecosystem and color the squares according to the key below.

grasshoppers = brown   lizards = yellow   grass = green   hawks = red

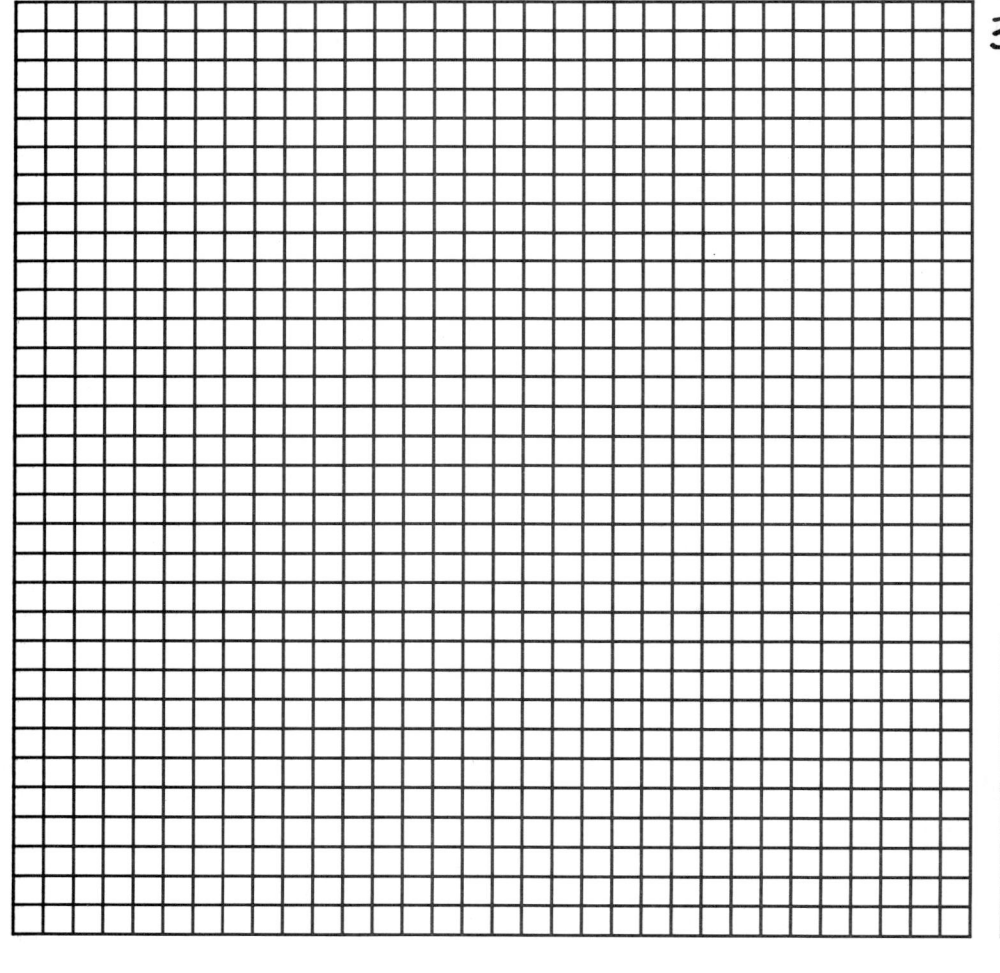

3. Make a mobile by cutting out the squares and connecting them with a piece of thread.

"Try and catch me!"

CRITTERS   138   ©1989 AIMS Education Foundation

CENSUS TAKERS

I. **Topic Area**
   Population sampling

II. **Introductory Statement**
   Students will take samples of a critter population and estimate the total population from the samples.

III. **Math Skills**   **Science Processes**
   a. Sampling   a. Predicting
   b. Averaging   b. Generalizing
   c. Graphing

IV. **Materials**
   activity sheets
   scissors

V. **Key Question**
   How can you find the population of a large number of animals?

VI. **Background Information**
   Knowing the population of an organism is important in studying it. Many times it is very difficult or impossible to count a large population of organisms. To get a good idea of the total population of an organism scientists determine the area the organism occupies. They then count the number of organisms in random, small sections of the larger area. The numbers of organisms in the samples are then averaged to find the average number of organisms living in a unit area. This unit area varies with the size and range of the organism being studied; for large organisms with a big range the unit might be square kilometers, for smaller organisms, square meters and for even smaller organisms, square centimeters or millimeters. When the average number of organisms per unit area is found, it is used to estimate the total population by multiplying the number of organisms in the unit area by the total area the organism occupies. This gives scientists a fairly accurate population estimate for a given organism.

VII. **Management Suggestions**
   1. Students can work in small groups or individually.
   2. Demonstrate how to cut the center square out of the sampling square.
   3. Students should only count *whole or nearly whole critters* within the cut out square when they take their samples.
   4. Students may count the actual number of critters on the sheet after taking their samples and estimating or be given the correct number (393).

VIII. **Procedure**
   1. Introduce the concept of sampling. This might be done by asking the class how many students are in their school and brainstorming ways that they could find out. Discuss ways to get an answer without counting every student. Students could then do a population study of the school by finding the average number of students per class by counting a few classes and averaging (sampling) and multiplying that number times the number of classes in the school. Compare the results from this method to the actual count from the office.
   2. Distribute the activity sheet with the critters drawn on it and have students predict the total number of critters.
   3. Pass out the second activity sheet and have each student record their prediction. Have students cut out their sampling square and use it to take five samples of the population. Be sure the samples are randomly taken. Students may drop the cut out square on the critter sheet or close their eyes and place it on the sheet. Students record the number of critters counted in each sample and calculate the average number of critters in a square unit. They multiply the average number of critters for the sample square unit by 63, since the critter population inhabits an area of 63 square units (7x9).
   4. Compare the population estimates to the actual count (393 critters) and find the difference.
   5. Record each group member's population estimates on the board and make a line graph.
   6. Using a different color crayon or pencil, draw a straight line on the graph to represent the actual number of critters. Have the students compare their estimates to the line representing the actual number.
   7. Using the group estimates, find the class average of the population estimates and compare it to the actual count.

IX. **Discussion Questions**
   1. Why is it important to select a random sample?
   2. How did the population estimates and the actual population differ?
   3. Do you think this is an accurate way to determine the population of a large area?
   4. Why would this be a particularly good method for finding whale populations?
   5. How is a real plot study different from our classroom activity?
   6. How does the class average compare to the actual population?

X. **Extended Activities**
   1. Sprinkle sand on a sheet of graph paper and take several samples and find the approximate number of grains on the whole sheet.
   2. Have students do a plot study of a local area.

XI. **Curriculum Coordinates**
   Art:
   Students can color in the activity sheet attempting to camouflage the critters.
   Geography:
   Discuss local plants and animals that could be used to do a census.
   Science:
   Discuss how plot studies may differ at different times of the day and during different seasons.

CENSUS TAKERS

Name________________

1) Prediction ________

2) Population Samples

A ________

B ________

C ________

D ________

E ________

3) Sample Total ________

4) Average (÷ 5) ________

5) X Number of Square Units ________

6) Population Estimate ________

7) Actual Population ________

8) Difference ________

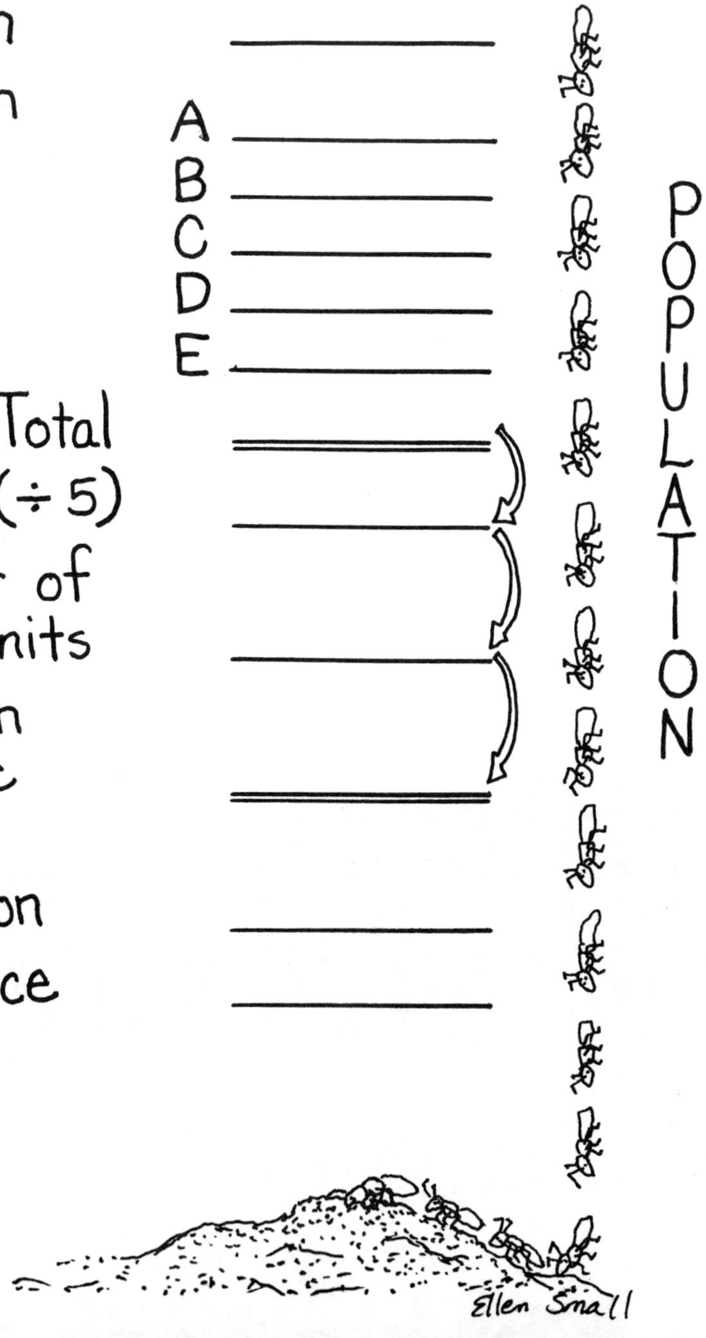

POPULATION
Ellen Small

Population Estimates

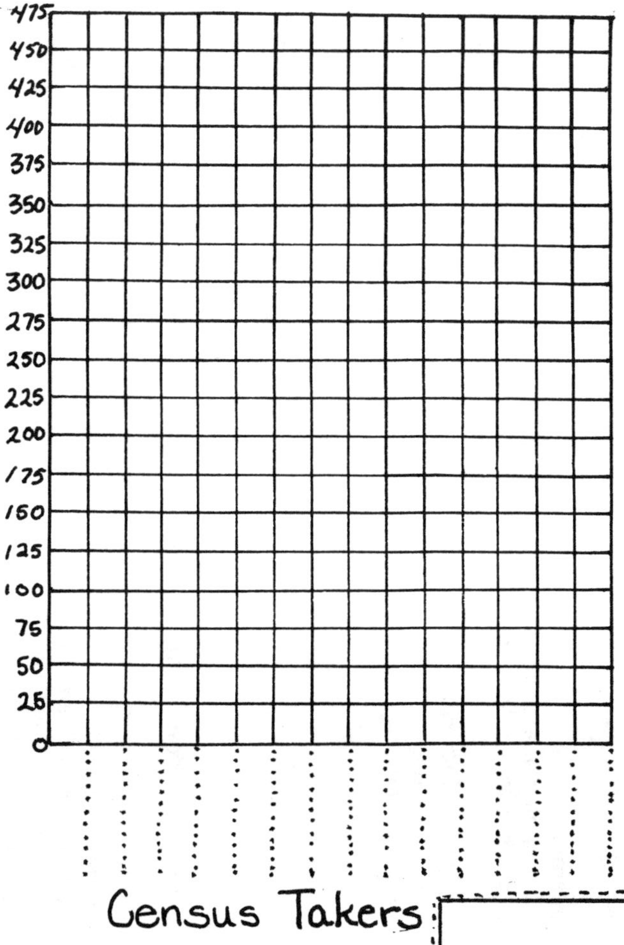

475
450
425
400
375
350
325
300
275
250
225
200
175
150
125
100
75
50
25
0
Census Takers

Cut Out

©1989 AIMS Education Foundation

CENSUS TAKERS

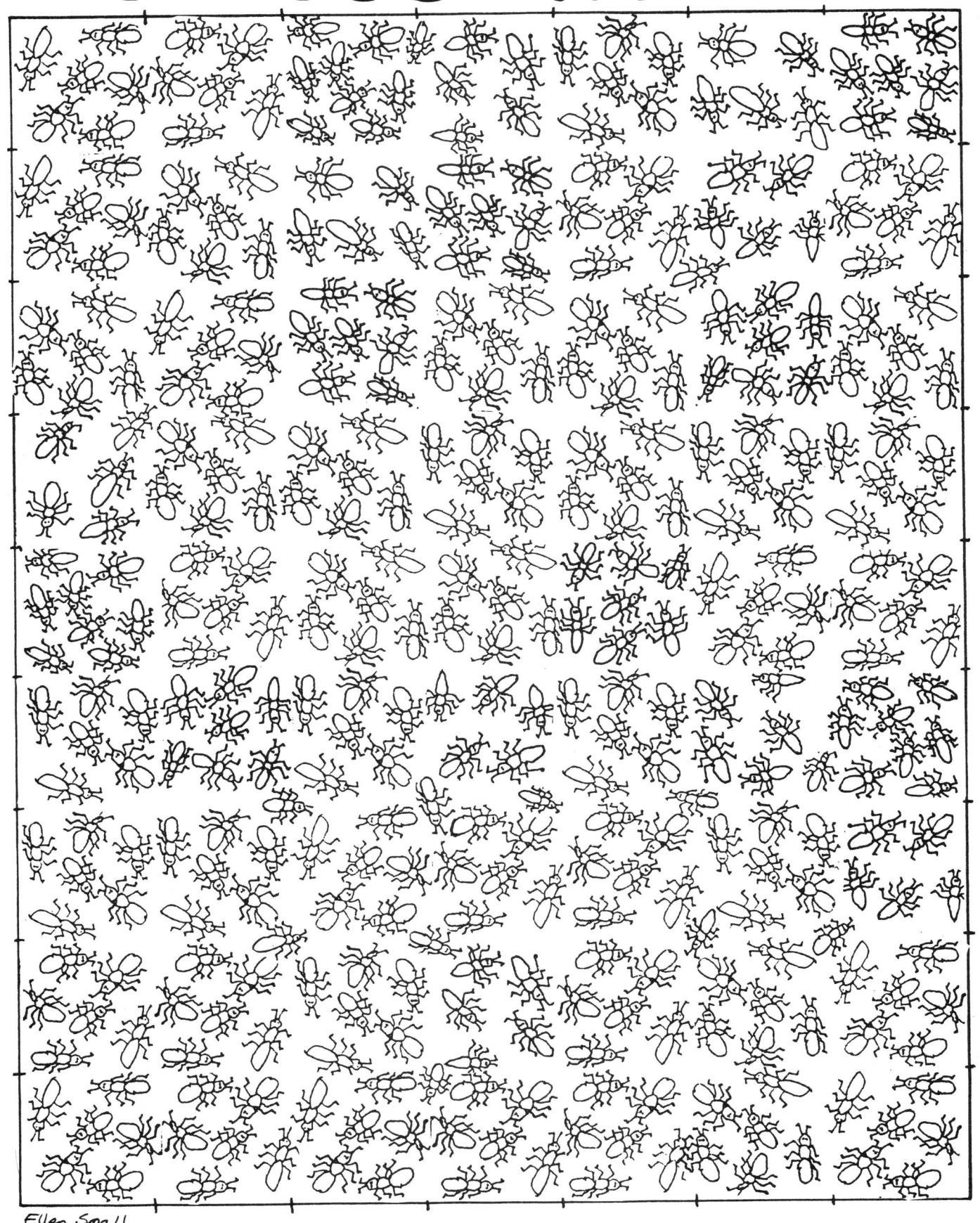

WHO'S HOME IN THE BIOME?

I. Topic Area
Biomes

II. Introductory Statement
Students will review which plants and animals are found in each biome by playing a board game.

III. Math Skills   Science Processes
  a. Observing
  b. Classifying
  c. Collecting
  d. Organizing data

IV. Materials
Per group of 4:
  4 biome data cards
  1 sheet of biome plant/animal record cards
  32 blank playing cards
    (8 cards per person to draw and label any plants or animals from their biome.)
    (3 x 5 cards work well)
  pencils
  crayons
  colored markers

V. Key Question
How are the plants and animals living in a particular biome adapted to the climatic and geographical features of that biome?

VI. Background Information
A biome is an area that is comprised of similar geographical and climatic features, with rainfall and temperature being particularly important. It is also characterized by the distinctive life forms of plants and animals that inhabit it. The location of biomes on a world map will show a latitudinal and altitudinal succession. Because of the impact of climate, certain types of producers will flourish, as will the consumers in their food chain. Thus, biomes are often identified by the plants and animals that inhabit them. This lesson will focus on six land biomes and two water biomes. Some sources break down the biomes further, listing more land and marine biomes. The eight biomes covered in this activity are detailed on the biome data cards.

VII. Management Suggestions
1. This game is most useful as a follow-up or reinforcement activity for a Biome unit. It can be played over and over again. Playing cards can be saved in baggies and reused.
2. Cut out the biome plant and animal record cards before starting the game.
3. If students have a hard time drawing the plants and animals on the blank playing cards, they can paste pictures of plants and animals cut from old magazines on the blank cards instead. The playing cards should be labeled with the name of the plant or animal.
4. You may want to study and discuss the world biome map before playing the game.

VIII. Procedure
1. Place students in groups of four.
2. Each student selects or is assigned one of the eight biomes.
3. Students read their biome data card and choose eight plants and/or animals that live in that biome.
4. Students record these eight choices on their biome record card and draw pictures of plants and animals chosen on the blank playing cards. They will label these pictures. Students can also use cutout pictures of plants and animals.
5. Explain the rules and begin play.

Rules:
1. Shuffle all the group's plant and animal playing cards together.
2. Deal three playing cards to each player and place the rest in a pile in the center of the group, face down.
3. First player asks any other player for a plant or animal from his biome record card. If the player asked has it, he must give it to that player. First player can then go again. If the player asked does not have the card, player says "go search." First player then draws one card from the pile and the next player takes a turn.
4. Play continues until someone collects five cards listed on their biome record card and calls out "Biome".

IX. Discussion Questions
1. Did anyone have the same plant or animal as another player?
2. How is it possible for a plant or animal to live in more than one biome?
3. What plants and animals are restricted to a single biome?
4. Which biomes have the most limited selection of plants and animals? Why?

X. Extended Activities
1. Have students find out what biome they live in and find additional native plants and animals that live there.
2. Study the world biome map. Use a blank map to draw in one of the eight biomes studied.

XI. Curriculum Coordinates
Drama:
Do a puppet show that teaches about a biome.
Language Arts:
Interview your favorite animal and find out all about its biome.
Art:
Make a three dimensional model or diorama of a biome.
Geography:
Research what biomes you would travel through if you traveled from the North Pole to the South Pole. Is there a pattern?

CRITTERS   ©1989 AIMS Education Foundation

Name _____

Grasslands: The grasslands are often known by other names such as steppes, plains, pampas, savannahs and veldts depending upon where they are located. Grasslands can be found in Africa, Australia, North America, South America and Asia. These areas get between 25-75 cm of rain per year and produce all kinds of grasses, wheat and corn. The animals that live there are mostly plant eaters like gophers, rabbits, giraffes, gazelles, buffalo and antelope. In North America bison used to be found on the grasslands. A variety of birds live on the grasslands. Some of them are ring necked pheasants, meadowlarks and prairie chickens.

Taiga: The taiga or coniferous forest is probably the world's largest land biome. It is located south of the tundra and stretches across portions of North America, Europe and Asia. During the summers, the soil remains very wet and is suitable for lichens and mosses. Fir and spruce trees grow well in this environment. The trees provide homes for many birds including the crossbill, which is capable of cracking cones to eat the seeds. A variety of animals are found in the taiga. They include moose, weasels, wolves, deer, lynx, caribou, porcupines, beaver, mink and bears.

CRITTERS

Tundra: The tundra is the coldest biome. It is found around the Arctic Circle and portions of Antarctica. The tundra gets very little precipitation and most of its water comes from snow. Although there is some thawing, a layer called permafrost, remains permanently frozen year round. Because of the severe weather conditions there are limited producers. These include lichens, reindeer moss, true mosses, and some low shrubs and sedges. Trees cannot establish root systems through the permafrost. Although there is a variety of animal life, many animals live in the tundra only during the summer. Caribou, polar bears, foxes, snowshoe hares, mice, and moles can be found there. Flies and mosquitoes have adapted their life cycles to the extremes of the tundra weather and live in the tundra year round.

Tropical Rain Forest: The tropical rain forest is found around the equator where temperatures are about 25°C all year, and there is an average rainfall of 200 cm. Portions of South America, Central America, Central Asia, Australia and Africa are included in the biome. Because of the humid conditions, this biome has the greatest amount of plant growth. Large trees, such as banyans, wild figs and mahogany form a canopy that prevents much light from reaching the ground. Other plants like bromeliads and lianas live in the canopy. Many of the animals also live in the trees. Bats, squirrels, monkeys, tree frogs and sloths are found here. On the ground there are beetles, spiders, snakes and antelopes.

Freshwater Biome: Fresh water all over the world makes up this biome. It includes rivers, lakes, streams and ponds. Algae is a plant common to all these bodies of water. Elodea, duckweed and water lilies are other freshwater plants. Many animals live in the water as well as the shoreline. Beaver, trout, frogs, turtles, crayfish, snails, salamanders, mosquitoes, dragonflies and perch are found in the freshwater biome.

Deserts: Deserts are a result of very little annual rainfall, usually less than 25 cm per year. Not all deserts are hot. Deserts are found in the United States, Africa, Asia, Australia, India and South America. Plants and animals have developed special adaptations for living in this environment. Plants like cacti and yucca trees are spaced far apart and have either little surface area, good water storage or a strong root system. Jack rabbits, kangaroo rats, gila monsters and rattlesnakes have also adapted. Many animals are able to tolerate the heat because they estivate or "sleep" during the heat and move about at night. Owls, hawks and scorpions are other desert residents.

Saltwater Biome: The ocean biome is the largest of all biomes since approximately 7/10ths of the earth is water and most of that is salt water. Any water environment that has at least 3.5% salt is considered salt water. Scientists divide the ocean into smaller biomes by amount of light and temperature. Algae, bacteria and seaweed are found in salt water. The animals found in the ocean are varied depending upon where they live. Clams, crabs, barnacles, flounders, mussels, oysters, sea cucumbers and stingrays live close to shore. In the ocean there are whales, sharks, swordfish, octopi, sea lions, dolphins and tuna. The ocean is the only biome that insects do not live in, although they may fly over its surface.

Temperate Forests: The temperate forest consists of areas that have an annual rainfall of 100 cm per year. These areas are found in North America, South America, Asia and Europe. This biome has four distinct seasons but rarely has a snowcover all winter. Many trees, including beeches, maples, oaks and hickories grow in the temperate forest. All of these trees lose their leaves during the fall. Visitors will find worms, insects, salamanders and snakes on the ground. Mammals include squirrels, raccoons, rabbits, skunks, opossums, bears and deer.

Ecologist: _____

Biome: _____

1. _____
2. _____
3. _____
4. _____
5. _____
6. _____
7. _____
8. _____

Ecologist: _____

Biome: _____

1. _____
2. _____
3. _____
4. _____
5. _____
6. _____
7. _____
8. _____

Ecologist: _____

Biome: _____

1. _____
2. _____
3. _____
4. _____
5. _____
6. _____
7. _____
8. _____

Ecologist: _____

Biome: _____

1. _____
2. _____
3. _____
4. _____
5. _____
6. _____
7. _____
8. _____

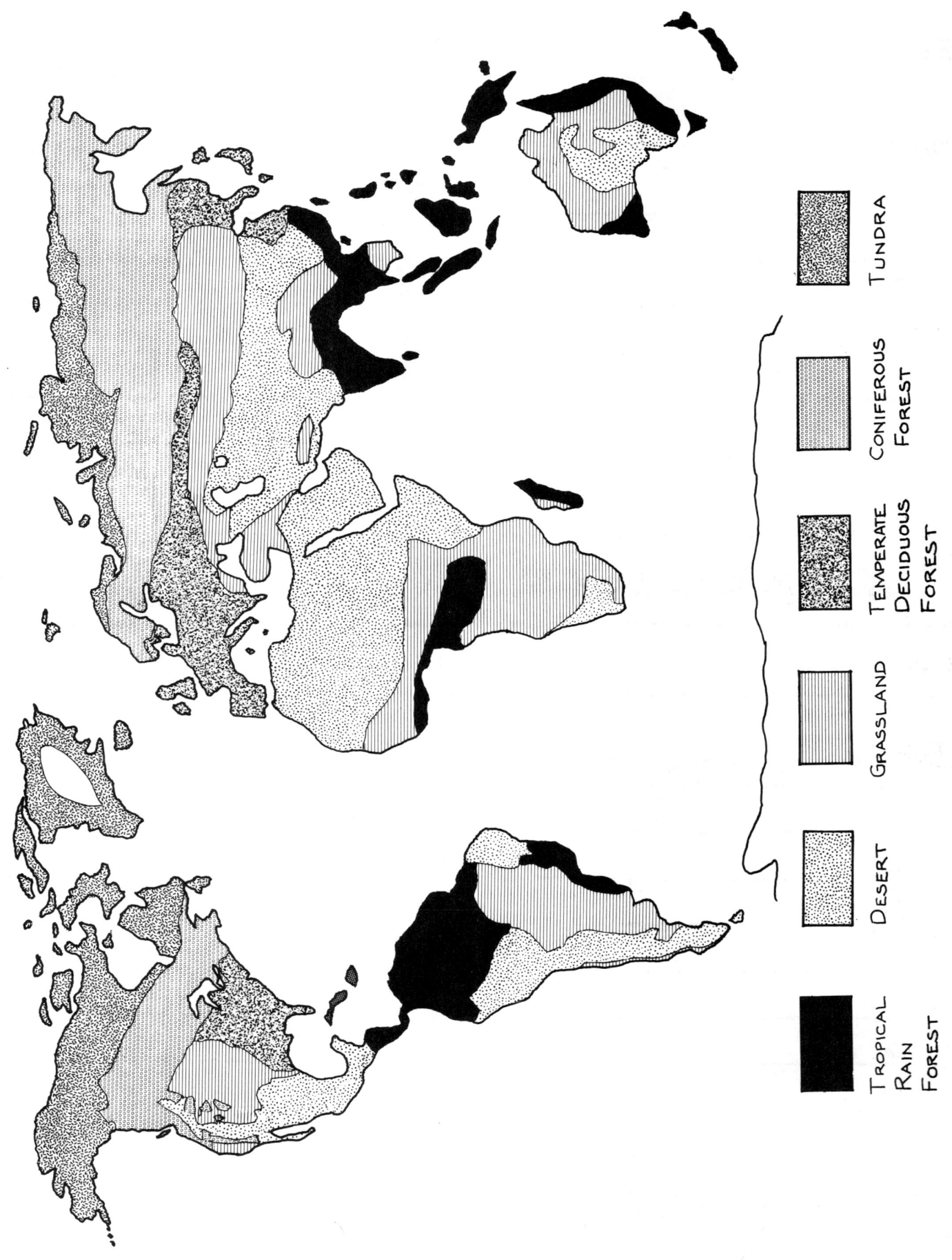

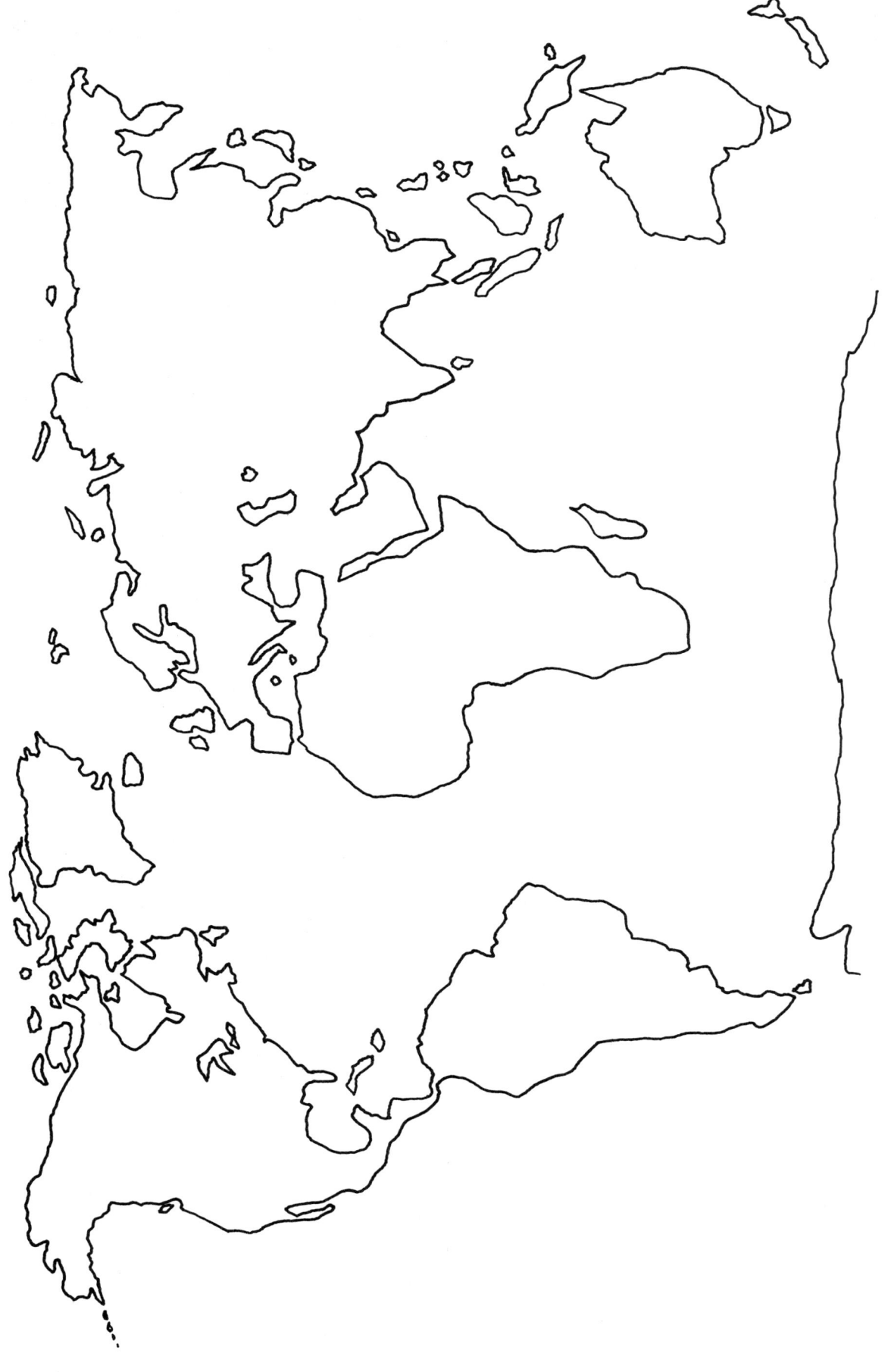

CRITTERS

Critter Trivia Ideas

Read one trivia card each day and place it on the calendar.

Make up questions using trivia cards - ask them in a "game show" format.

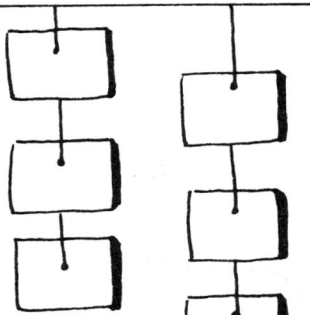

Make a mobile

Trivia Charades

Have students come up with new ways to use these cards.

CRITTERS 150 ©1989 AIMS Education Foundation

Critter Trivia

There are more than 250,000 kinds of beetles. *Is that true?*

Earthworms have no eyes. *I need glasses.*

People used to think pillbugs were "good medicine" and swallowed them like pills. *Don't swallow me!*

40,000 silkworm eggs weigh approximately one ounce.

The giant African snail grows to about 6". *You're huge!*

Fairyflies are so tiny that 2 of them can fit on a period. *Are we that little?*

Insects never close their eyes because they have no eyelids. *How can we sleep?*

An ant's compound eye is made of 50 small eyes. *"Eye" can't believe it!*

Insects do not live in saltwater. *Save me!*

A mother turbot fish can lay 9,000,000 eggs.  "That's alot of eggs!"	 There are more insects than all other kinds of animals put together.
 "That sounds like hard work!" Bees can pull loads 300x their own weight	There are 3,000 types of cockroaches but only 17 carry diseases.
The Chinese were the first to discover silk. 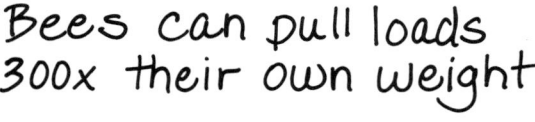	A Mudskipper fish has the head of a frog. 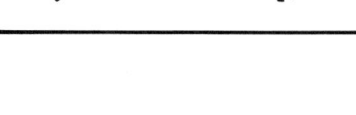 "Croak Croak"
Some spiders catch small fish and insects in freshwater ponds.  "Oh no! not me"	Some freshwater snails have gills and some have lungs.  "Very Interesting!"
In Africa there is a type of beetle called Goliath that grows to 5-6 inches.  "You're sure big!"	 "What shall I wear today?" Prawns, sole and chameleons can all change their color for camouflage.

CRITTERS

The AIMS Program

AIMS is the acronym for "Activities Integrating Mathematics and Science." Such integration enriches learning and makes it meaningful and holistic. AIMS began as a project of Fresno Pacific University to integrate the study of mathematics and science in grades K-9, but has since expanded to include language arts, social studies, and other disciplines.

AIMS is a continuing program of the non-profit AIMS Education Foundation. It had its inception in a National Science Foundation funded program whose purpose was to explore the effectiveness of integrating mathematics and science. The project directors in cooperation with 80 elementary classroom teachers devoted two years to a thorough field-testing of the results and implications of integration.

The approach met with such positive results that the decision was made to launch a program to create instructional materials incorporating this concept. Despite the fact that thoughtful educators have long recommended an integrative approach, very little appropriate material was available in 1981 when the project began. A series of writing projects have ensued and today the AIMS Education Foundation is committed to continue the creation of new integrated activities on a permanent basis.

The AIMS program is funded through the sale of this developing series of books and proceeds from the Foundation's endowment. All net income from program and products flows into a trust fund administered by the AIMS Education Foundation. Use of these funds is restricted to support of research, development, and publication of new materials. Writers donate all their rights to the Foundation to support its on-going program. No royalties are paid to the writers.

The rationale for integration lies in the fact that science, mathematics, language arts, social studies, etc., are integrally interwoven in the real world from which it follows that they should be similarly treated in the classroom where we are preparing students to live in that world. Teachers who use the AIMS program give enthusiastic endorsement to the effectiveness of this approach.

Science encompasses the art of questioning, investigating, hypothesizing, discovering, and communicating. Mathematics is the language that provides clarity, objectivity, and understanding. The language arts provide us powerful tools of communication. Many of the major contemporary societal issues stem from advancements in science and must be studied in the context of the social sciences. Therefore, it is timely that all of us take seriously a more holistic mode of educating our students. This goal motivates all who are associated with the AIMS Program. We invite you to join us in this effort.

Meaningful integration of knowledge is a major recommendation coming from the nation's professional science and mathematics associations. The American Association for the Advancement of Science in *Science for All Americans* strongly recommends the integration of mathematics, science, and technology. The National Council of Teachers of Mathematics places strong emphasis on applications of mathematics such as are found in science investigations. AIMS is fully aligned with these recommendations.

Extensive field testing of AIMS investigations confirms these beneficial results.

1. Mathematics becomes more meaningful, hence more useful, when it is applied to situations that interest students.
2. The extent to which science is studied and understood is increased, with a significant economy of time, when mathematics and science are integrated.
3. There is improved quality of learning and retention, supporting the thesis that learning which is meaningful and relevant is more effective.
4. Motivation and involvement are increased dramatically as students investigate real-world situations and participate actively in the process.

We invite you to become part of this classroom teacher movement by using an integrated approach to learning and sharing any suggestions you may have. The AIMS Program welcomes you!

© 1999 AIMS Education Foundation

AIMS Education Foundation Programs

A Day with AIMS

Intensive one-day workshops are offered to introduce educators to the philosophy and rationale of AIMS. Participants will discuss the methodology of AIMS and the strategies by which AIMS principles may be incorporated into curriculum. Each participant will take part in a variety of hands-on AIMS investigations to gain an understanding of such aspects as the scientific/mathematical content, classroom management, and connections with other curricular areas. *A Day with AIMS* workshops may be offered anywhere in the United States. Necessary supplies and take-home materials are usually included in the enrollment fee.

A Week with AIMS

Throughout the nation, AIMS offers many one-week workshops each year, usually in the summer. Each workshop lasts five days and includes at least 30 hours of AIMS hands-on instruction. Participants are grouped according to the grade level(s) in which they are interested. Instructors are members of the AIMS Instructional Leadership Network. Supplies for the activities and a generous supply of take-home materials are included in the enrollment fee. Sites are selected on the basis of applications submitted by educational organizations. If chosen to host a workshop, the host agency agrees to provide specified facilities and cooperate in the promotion of the workshop. The AIMS Education Foundation supplies workshop materials as well as the travel, housing, and meals for instructors.

AIMS One-Week Perspectives Workshops

Each summer, Fresno Pacific University offers AIMS one-week workshops on its campus in Fresno, California. AIMS Program Directors and highly qualified members of the AIMS National Leadership Network serve as instructors.

The Science Festival and the Festival of Mathematics

Each summer, Fresno Pacific University offers a Science Festival and a Festival of Mathematics. These festivals have gained national recognition as inspiring and challenging experiences, giving unique opportunities to experience hands-on mathematics and science in topical and grade-level groups. Guest faculty includes some of the nation's most highly regarded mathematics and science educators. Supplies and take-home materials are included in the enrollment fee.

The AIMS Instructional Leadership Program

This is an AIMS staff-development program seeking to prepare facilitators for leadership roles in science/math education in their home districts or regions. Upon successful completion of the program, trained facilitators may become members of the AIMS Instructional Leadership Network, qualified to conduct AIMS workshops, teach AIMS in-service courses for college credit, and serve as AIMS consultants. Intensive training is provided in mathematics, science, process and thinking skills, workshop management, and other relevant topics.

College Credit and Grants

Those who participate in workshops may often qualify for college credit. If the workshop takes place on the campus of Fresno Pacific University, that institution may grant appropriate credit. If the workshop takes place off-campus, arrangements can sometimes be made for credit to be granted by another college or university. In addition, the applicant's home school district is often willing to grant in-service or professional development credit. Many educators who participate in AIMS workshops are recipients of various types of educational grants, either local or national. Nationally known foundations and funding agencies have long recognized the value of AIMS mathematics and science workshops to educators. The AIMS Education Foundation encourages educators interested in attending or hosting workshops to explore the possibilities suggested above. Although the Foundation strongly supports such interest, it reminds applicants that they have the primary responsibility for fulfilling *current* requirements.

For current information regarding the programs described above, please complete the following:

Information Request

Please send current information on the items checked:

___ *Basic Information Packet* on AIMS materials
___ *Festival of Mathematics*
___ *Science Festival*
___ *AIMS Instructional Leadership Program*

___ *AIMS One-Week Perspectives* workshops
___ *A Week with AIMS* workshops
___ Hosting information for *A Day with AIMS* workshops
___ Hosting information for *A Week with AIMS* workshops

Name _____ Phone _____

Address _____
         Street   City   State   Zip

© 1999 AIMS Education Foundation

AIMS Program Publications

GRADES K-4 SERIES

Bats Incredible
Brinca de Alegria Hacia la Primavera con las Matemáticas y Ciencias
Cáete de Gusto Hacia el Otoño con la Matemáticas y Ciencias
Cycles of Knowing and Growing
Fall Into Math and Science
Field Detectives
Glide Into Winter With Math and Science
Hardhatting in a Geo-World (Revised Edition, 1996)
Jaw Breakers and Heart Thumpers (Revised Edition, 1995)
Los Cincos Sentidos
Overhead and Underfoot (Revised Edition, 1994)
Patine al Invierno con Matemáticas y Ciencias
Popping With Power (Revised Edition, 1996)
Primariamente Física (Revised Edition, 1994)
Primarily Earth
Primariamente Plantas
Primarily Physics (Revised Edition, 1994)
Primarily Plants
Sense-able Science
Spring Into Math and Science
Under Construction

GRADES K-6 SERIES

Budding Botanist
Critters
El Botanista Principiante
Exploring Environments
Mostly Magnets
Ositos Nada Más
Primarily Bears
Principalmente Imanes
Water Precious Water

GRADES 5-9 SERIES

Actions with Fractions
Brick Layers
Conexiones Eléctricas
Down to Earth
Electrical Connections
Finding Your Bearings (Revised Edition, 1996)
Floaters and Sinkers (Revised Edition, 1995)
From Head to Toe
Fun With Foods
Gravity Rules!
Historical Connections in Mathematics, Volume I
Historical Connections in Mathematics, Volume II
Historical Connections in Mathematics, Volume III
Machine Shop
Magnificent Microworld Adventures
Math + Science, A Solution
Off the Wall Science: A Poster Series Revisited
Our Wonderful World
Out of This World (Revised Edition, 1994)
Pieces and Patterns, A Patchwork in Math and Science
Piezas y Diseños, un Mosaic de Matemáticas y Ciencias
Soap Films and Bubbles
Spatial Visualization
The Sky's the Limit (Revised Edition, 1994)
The Amazing Circle, Volume 1
Through the Eyes of the Explorers:
    Minds-on Math & Mapping
What's Next, Volume 1
What's Next, Volume 2
What's Next, Volume 3

For further information write to:
AIMS Education Foundation • P.O. Box 8120 • Fresno, California 93747-8120

© 1999 AIMS Education Foundation

We invite you to subscribe to AIMS!

Each issue of *AIMS* contains a variety of material useful to educators at all grade levels. Feature articles of lasting value deal with topics such as mathematical or science concepts, curriculum, assessment, the teaching of process skills, and historical background. Several of the latest AIMS math/science investigations are always included, along with their reproducible activity sheets. As needs direct and space allows, various issues contain news of current developments, such as workshop schedules, activities of the AIMS Instructional Leadership Network, and announcements of upcoming publications.

AIMS is published monthly, August through May. Subscriptions are on an annual basis only. A subscription entered at any time will begin with the next issue, but will also include the previous issues of that volume. Readers have preferred this arrangement because articles and activities within an annual volume are often interrelated.

Please note that an *AIMS* subscription automatically includes duplication rights for one school site for all issues included in the subscription. Many schools build cost-effective library resources with their subscriptions.

YES! I am interested in subscribing to AIMS.

Name _____   Home Phone _____

Address _____   City, State, Zip _____

Please send the following volumes (subject to availability):

_____ Volume V   (1990-91) $30.00   _____ Volume X   (1995-96) $30.00
_____ Volume VI   (1991-92) $30.00   _____ Volume XI   (1996-97) $30.00
_____ Volume VII   (1992-93) $30.00   _____ Volume XII   (1997-98) $30.00
_____ Volume IX   (1994-95) $30.00   _____ Volume XIII   (1998-99) $30.00

_____ **Limited offer: Volumes XIII & XIV (1998-2000) $55.00**
(Note: Prices may change without notice)

Check your method of payment:

❏ Check enclosed in the amount of $ _____
❏ Purchase order attached (Please include the P.O.#, the authorizing signature, and position of the authorizing person.)
❏ Credit Card   ❏ Visa   ❏ MasterCard   Amount $ _____
   Card # _____   Expiration Date _____
   Signature _____   Today's Date _____

Make checks payable to **AIMS Education Foundation**.
Mail to *AIMS* Magazine, P.O. Box 8120, Fresno, CA 93747-8120.
Phone (559) 255-4094 or (888) 733-2467   FAX (559) 255-6396
AIMS Homepage: http://www.AIMSedu.org/

© 1999 AIMS Education Foundation

AIMS Duplication Rights Program

AIMS has received many requests from school districts for the purchase of unlimited duplication rights to AIMS materials. In response, the AIMS Education Foundation has formulated the program outlined below. There is a built-in flexibility which, we trust, will provide for those who use AIMS materials extensively to purchase such rights for either individual activities or entire books.

It is the goal of the AIMS Education Foundation to make its materials and programs available at reasonable cost. All income from the sale of publications and duplication rights is used to support AIMS programs; hence, strict adherence to regulations governing duplication is essential. Duplication of AIMS materials beyond limits set by copyright laws and those specified below is strictly forbidden.

Limited Duplication Rights

Any purchaser of an AIMS book may make up to *200 copies* of any activity in that book for use at *one school site*. Beyond that, rights must be purchased according to the appropriate category.

Unlimited Duplication Rights for Single Activities

An individual or school may purchase the right to make an unlimited number of copies of a single activity. The royalty is $5.00 per activity per school site.

Examples: 3 activities x 1 site x $5.00 = $15.00
9 activities x 3 sites x $5.00 = $135.00

Unlimited Duplication Rights for Entire Books

A school or district may purchase the right to make an unlimited number of copies of a single, *specified* book. The royalty is $20.00 per book per school site. This is in addition to the cost of the book.

Examples: 5 books x 1 site   x $20.00 = $100.00
12 books x 10 sites x $20.00 = $2400.00

Magazine/Newsletter Duplication Rights

Those who purchase *AIMS* (magazine)/*Newsletter* are hereby granted permission to make up to 200 copies of any portion of it, provided these copies will be used for educational purposes.

Workshop Instructors' Duplication Rights

Workshop instructors may distribute to registered workshop participants a maximum of 100 copies of any article and/or 100 copies of no more than eight activities, provided these six conditions are met:

1. Since all AIMS activities are based upon the *AIMS Model of Mathematics* and the *AIMS Model of Learning*, leaders must include in their presentations an explanation of these two models.
2. Workshop instructors must relate the AIMS activities presented to these basic explanations of the AIMS philosophy of education.
3. The copyright notice must appear on all materials distributed.
4. Instructors must provide information enabling participants to order books and magazines from the Foundation.
5. Instructors must inform participants of their limited duplication rights as outlined below.
6. Only student pages may be duplicated.

Written permission must be obtained for duplication beyond the limits listed above. Additional royalty payments may be required.

Workshop Participants' Rights

Those enrolled in workshops in which AIMS student activity sheets are distributed may duplicate a maximum of 35 copies or enough to use the lessons one time with one class, whichever is less. Beyond that, rights must be purchased according to the appropriate category.

Application for Duplication Rights

The purchasing agency or individual must clearly specify the following:
1. Name, address, and telephone number
2. Titles of the books for Unlimited Duplication Rights contracts
3. Titles of activities for Unlimited Duplication Rights contracts
4. Names and addresses of school sites for which duplication rights are being purchased.

NOTE: Books to be duplicated must be purchased separately and are not included in the contract for Unlimited Duplication Rights.

The requested duplication rights are automatically authorized when proper payment is received, although a *Certificate of Duplication Rights* will be issued when the application is processed.

Address all correspondence to: Contract Division
AIMS Education Foundation
P.O. Box 8120
Fresno, CA 93747-8120

© 1999 AIMS Education Foundation